The WORLD Around Us 2

An Integrated Science, Social Studies and Environmental Studies Book

To access digital content, please log in to **http://scholastic.co.in/en/products/twau/grade-2/sign-up**

Illustrations by Partha Sengupta and Durgadutt Pandey
Images: Shutterstock unless specified

Published by Scholastic India Pvt. Ltd.
A subsidiary of Scholastic Inc., New York, 10012 (USA).
Publishers since 1920, with international operations in Canada, Australia, New Zealand, the United Kingdom, India, and Hong Kong.

For information regarding permission, write to:
Scholastic India Pvt. Ltd.
A-27, Ground Floor, Bharti Sigma Centre
Infocity -1, Sector 34, Gurgaon (Haryana) 122001
Email: info_in@scholastic.asia

This edition: 2024
Reprinted 2025 (Twice)

ISBN-13: 978-81-8477-367-5

Contents

Introduction 4

1. My Body 7
2. My Family 15
3. My Home 20
4. My Neighbourhood 25
5. Time to Celebrate 35
6. Work and Play 44
7. Good Habits 48
8. Food 54
9. Clothes 61
10. Shelter 66
11. Communication and Transport 73
12. Directions and Maps 80
13. Safety 88
14. Living and Non-living Things 96
15. Plants 102
16. Animals 113
17. Our Universe 120
18. The Earth 130

Cross curricular project 140

Introduction

The World Around Us is a series of comprehensive environmental education course books for classes 1 to 5.

The books look at the child's natural, physical, and social environment. Within each level, lessons provide information from which basic concepts are deduced along with sufficient factual data, experiences and encouragement to enable them to generalise rationally about the environment.

This newly revised series is in accordance with the National Curriculum Framework (NCF) for School Education 2023, which has been adopted by the CBSE, ICSE and major state educational boards. It takes into consideration the curricular goals, competencies, and learning outcomes as illustrated by the NCF 2023.

Various sections in the books have been tagged to illustrate how the learning material adheres to the various skills and approaches recommended by the Framework.

In keeping with the spirit of advancement of technology in the field of education, the books exemplify how the 21st Century Skills of Information Literacy, Learning and Social skills have been interwoven into various tasks. Various exercises give students practice in using the scientific ways of learning and also using art to acquire information and express opinions. Consistent with the NEP's holistic approach to teaching and learning, the books raise awareness towards adopting sustainable practices for the environment and encourage cooperation amongst peers and in the society through various group and pair work tasks. The books follow the student-centered method of learning through discovery which ensures that the students learn about and relate to the concepts rather than memorise them.

Skill development

21st Century Skills

Communication

The skill of communication is engaging with others and exchanging ideas. Persons fluent in this skill are able to express thoughts and ideas clearly and coherently.

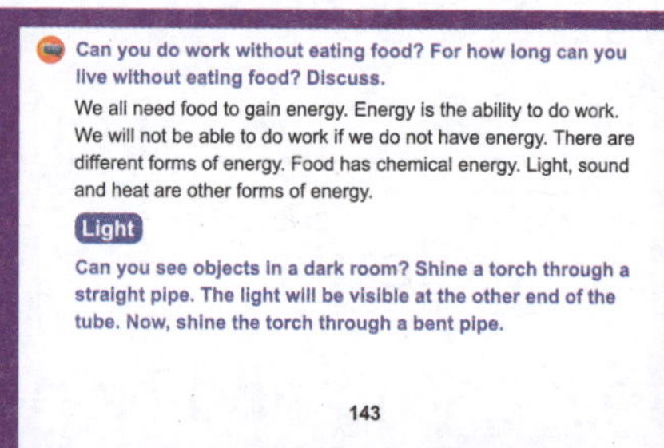

Can you do work without eating food? For how long can you live without eating food? Discuss.

We all need food to gain energy. Energy is the ability to do work. We will not be able to do work if we do not have energy. There are different forms of energy. Food has chemical energy. Light, sound and heat are other forms of energy.

Light

Can you see objects in a dark room? Shine a torch through a straight pipe. The light will be visible at the other end of the tube. Now, shine the torch through a bent pipe.

143

Creativity

It is the ability to use imagination and art, and think outside the box to solve problems for a more holistic understanding.

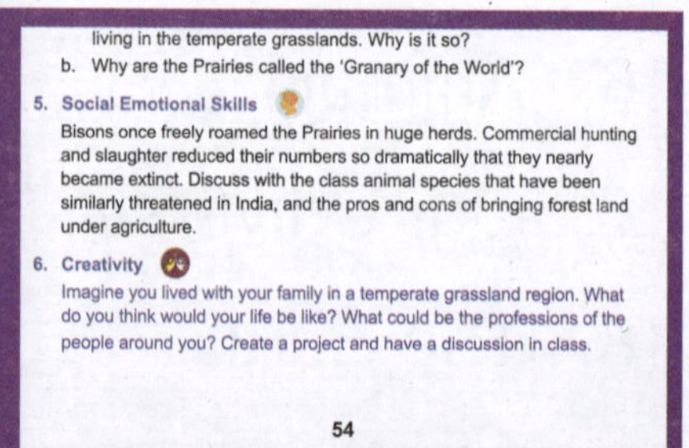

living in the temperate grasslands. Why is it so?

b. Why are the Prairies called the 'Granary of the World'?

5. **Social Emotional Skills**

Bisons once freely roamed the Prairies in huge herds. Commercial hunting and slaughter reduced their numbers so dramatically that they nearly became extinct. Discuss with the class animal species that have been similarly threatened in India, and the pros and cons of bringing forest land under agriculture.

6. **Creativity**

Imagine you lived with your family in a temperate grassland region. What do you think would your life be like? What could be the professions of the people around you? Create a project and have a discussion in class.

54

Critical thinking

It is the approach to analyse and use reasoning to solve problems.

(i) ears (ii) nose
(iii) tongue (iv) hands

(e) Which body part is being referred to in the given rhyme?
(i) stomach
(ii) hand
(iii) eyes
(iv) skin

Stretched smoothly tight,
Around my body day and night...
Largest part, that I own
Bigger than my brain or bone!

4. Critical thinking
(a) What would happen if one day you woke up with four hands? Discuss.

15

Social emotional skills

These are a person's ability to connect with those around them. It spans across interaction with friends, family, peers, coworkers, etc.

5. Social Emotional Skills
(a) As we grow, we do many things by ourselves, without any help from others. How do you feel when you do things on your own?
(b) Which of these things can you do on your own?

1. Tie my shoelaces	Yes/No
2. Wear my uniform	Yes/No
3. Comb my hair	Yes/No
4. Eat my food	Yes/No
5.Take water from the kitchen when required	Yes/No
6. Keep my things in place	Yes/No

Information literacy

These are a set of abilities required to recognise when information is needed and have the ability to locate, evaluate, and be able to effectively use the needed information.

Use an encyclopedia to find out what a 'bonsai' is.

Dispersal by explosion: Some plants, such as broom, peas and beans, have pods that explode as they ripen. This explosion helps to scatter the seeds.

broom

Dispersal by gravity: Large, heavy fruits, such as apples, just drop off the tree on to the ground as they ripen. These fruits can then be carried away from the parent plant by animals, by water or they might just simply roll away. Very often, their soft skin may burst open to scatter the seeds inside.

New Plants from Leaves, Stems and Roots

While new plants usually grow from seeds, they can also grow from the leaves, stems and roots of the parent plant.
New plants emerge from the roots of the dandelion plant.
Garlic is a special type of a stem. Cloves of a garlic can be used to grow a new plant.
The potato is also a stem, which has buds or 'eyes'. If we scoop out a part of the potato with a bud in it, it can be used to grow a new plant.

The 21st century skills help us in dealing with today's challenges. Meanwhile, the Sustainable Development Goals (SDGs) are a global framework that can guide us towards a sustainable future.

Sustainable Development Goals

These were adopted by the United Nations in 2015 as a universal call to action to end poverty and protect the planet. The 17 SDGs recognise that action in one area will affect outcomes in others, and that development must balance social, economic and environmental sustainability.

Discovery-oriented & Activity-based Learning

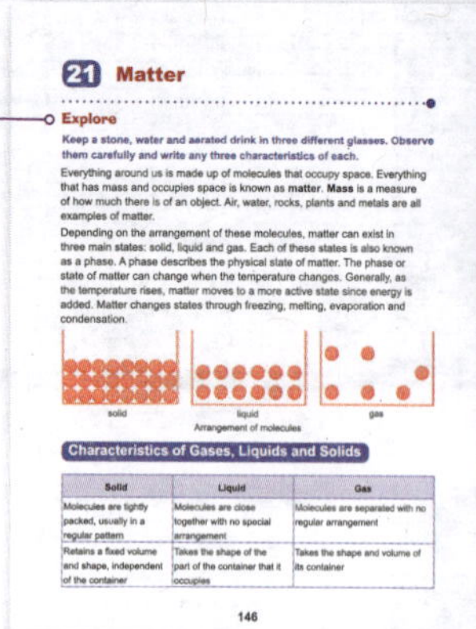

The **Explore** section gauges prior knowledge as well as builds curiosity.

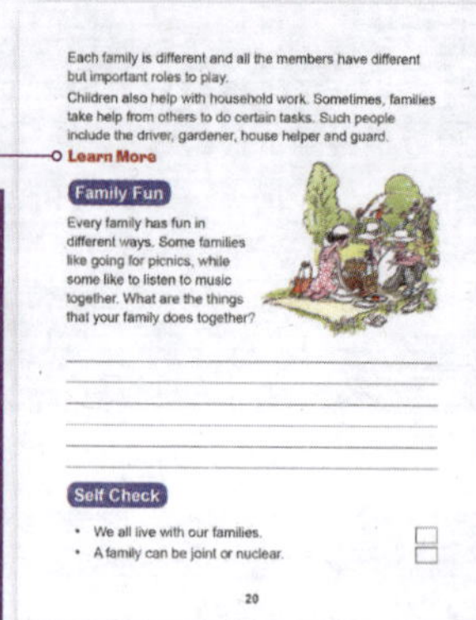

The **Learn More** section acts as an important educational tool to develop independent and critical thinking skills.

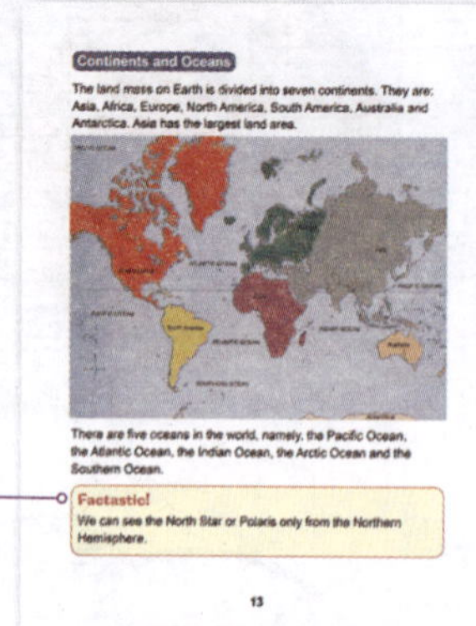

Relevant, interesting nuggets of information are presented in an easy-to-understand format in the **Factastic** section.

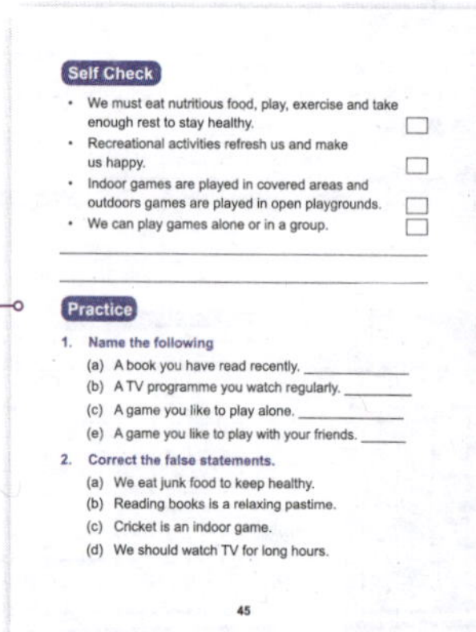

Exercises after every lesson to **evaluate** the students' progress.

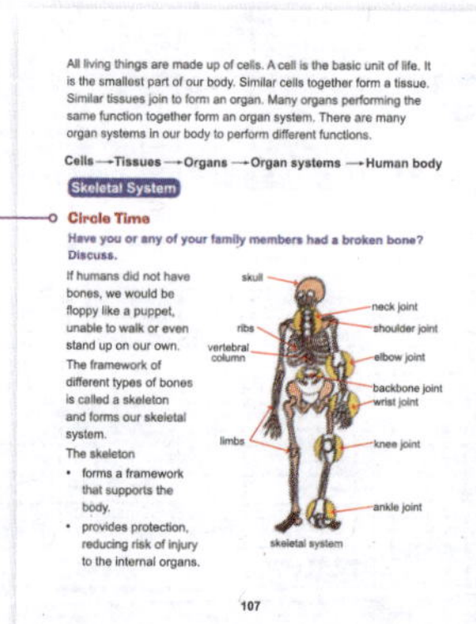

The **Circle Time** section sets out peer and group activities which further promote exchange of ideas while also laying the foundation for teamwork and ethics.

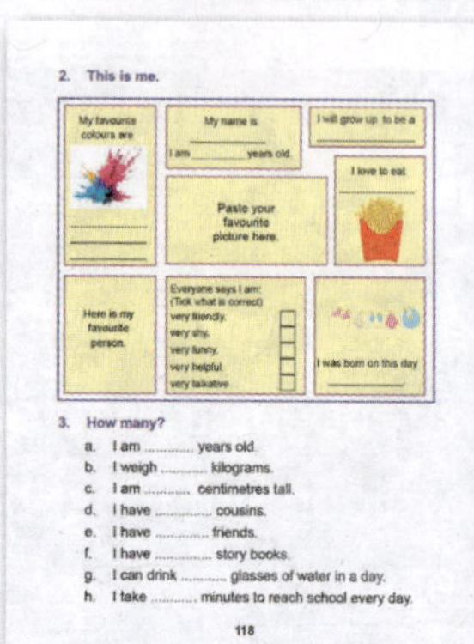

Cross curricular projects offer a creative way of researching information, collaborating and expressing yourself on a common theme between different subjects.

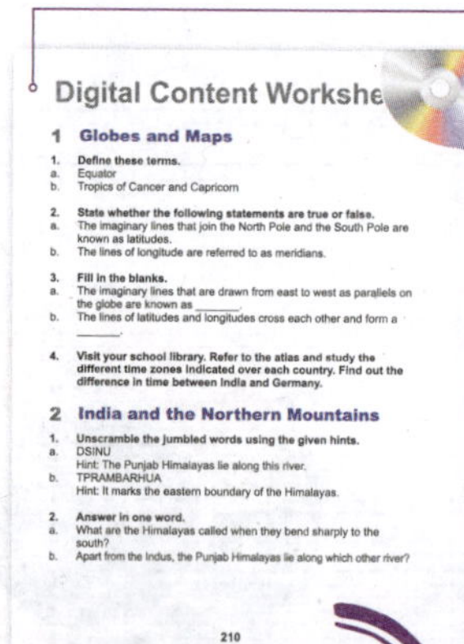

Exercises based on the educative videos and animations in the **Digital Content** to extend learning.

Scan me

1 My Body

Explore

How are you different from your friends?
Observe your friend and tick the correct boxes.

hair colour	brown	black
hair length	long	short
taller than me	yes	no
eye colour	brown	black

Though most human beings have similar bodies, it is important to remember that no two people look the same. Each person is different from the other. Each one of us is unique.

Everyone has different facial features.

Feature	Describing words	
face	round, long, oval	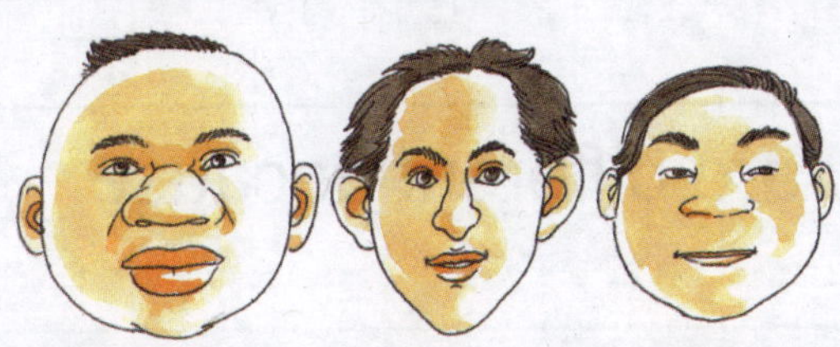
nose	long, flat, broad	
eyes	small, large, round	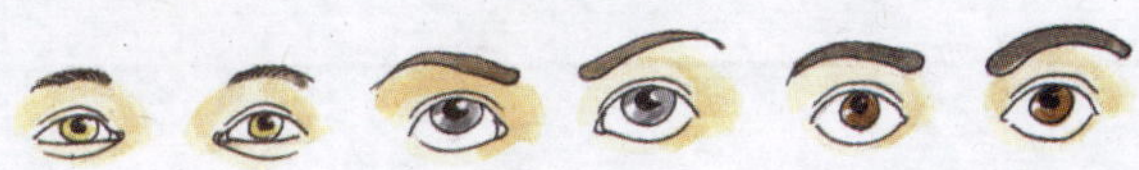

Use the describing words given in the box on the previous page to write about your friend's facial features.

____

____

Factastic!

Twins are persons who are born at the same time to the same mother. Often they look the same, and it is not easy to tell them apart. However, there are some twins who do not look like each other.

People from different countries look different from each other. There are about 8000 million people in the world. Each year, about 131 million more people are born.

Look at the picture on the right. These children are all different, but they are similar in some ways. They are similar because

____

____

They are different because ________________________

____

____

Internal Organs

The parts inside our bodies are known as **internal organs**.

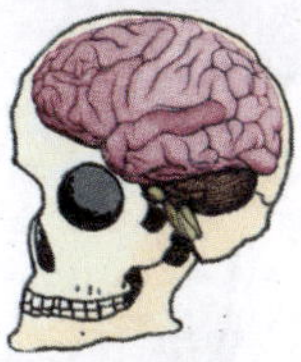

Our **brain** is inside our head.

It helps us to think, and it also controls the movements of our body. It is the control centre of the body.

Our **heart** is inside our chest. It beats all the time and pumps blood to all parts of our body.

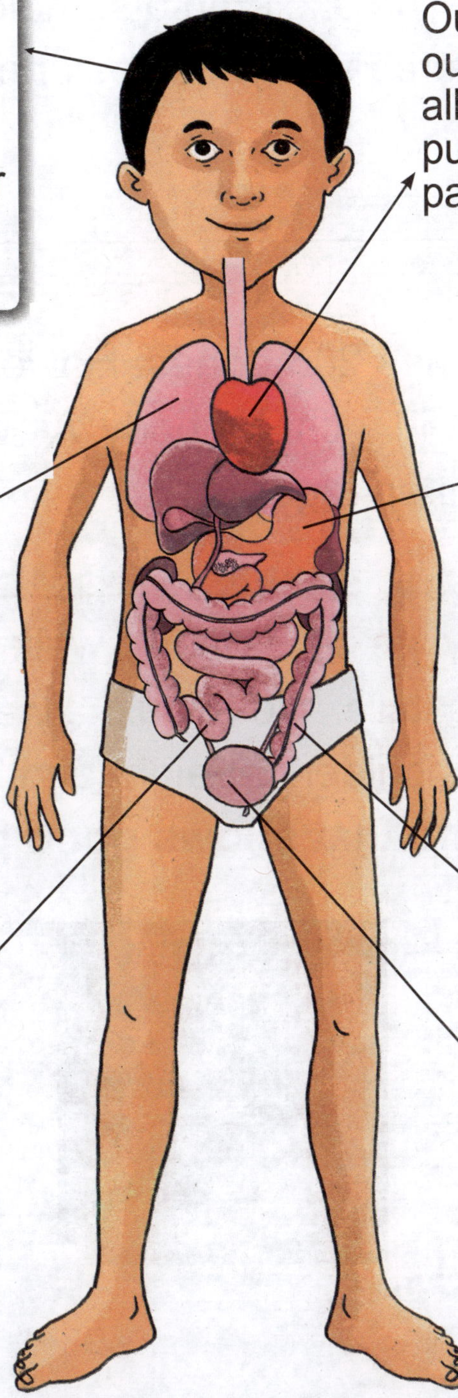

Our **lungs** help us to breathe.

Below the chest is our **stomach**. All the food that we eat goes into the stomach. Here it is churned and digested.

Our **large intestine**

Our **small intestine**

Our **urinary bladder**

Recall the names of external organs.

The Skeleton

Our body has a framework of bones known as the **skeleton**. The skeleton protects the internal organs of our body. (For example, the skull protects the brain. The skeleton also holds up the body.) It is covered with muscles and skin.

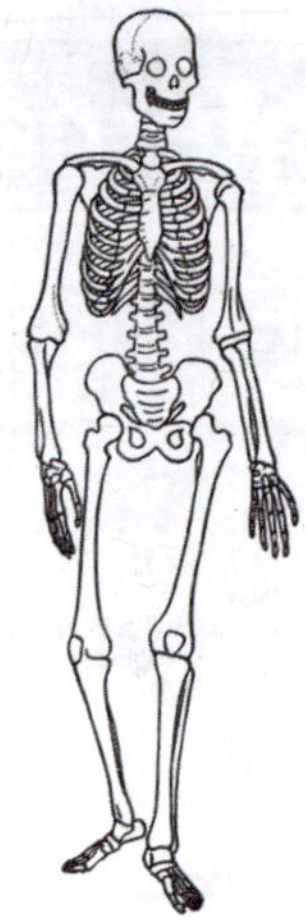

human skeleton

Factastic!

An adult human has 206 bones. However, there are about 300 bones in a child's body. As we grow, some of the bones get joined together.

Posture is the way we sit, stand or walk. We need to maintain proper posture. We should always walk and sit with our back upright, shoulders straight and head high.

Tick (✓) the picture that shows good posture.

 ☐

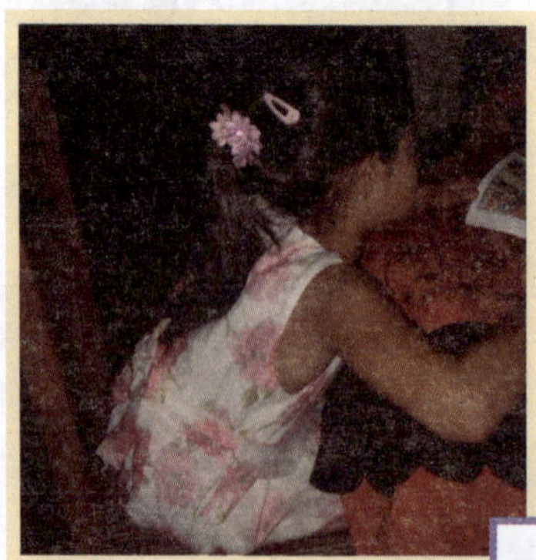 ☐

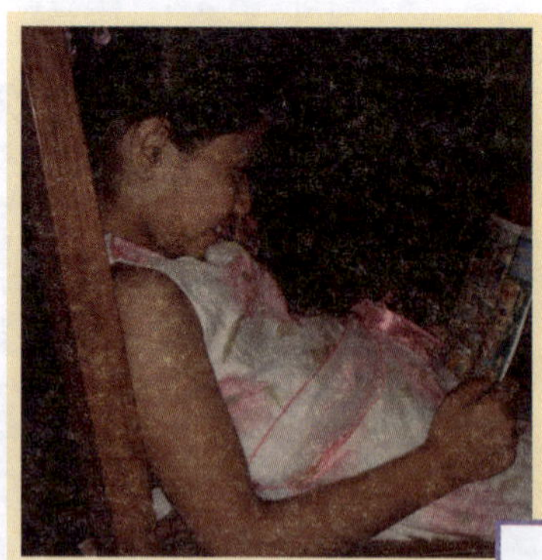 ☐

Circle Time

Discuss the importance of maintaining good posture.

Sense Organs

The eyes, ears, nose, tongue and skin are the five sense organs. They help us to see, hear, smell, taste and touch.

Sense of sight: We use our eyes to see what is happening around us.

Sense of hearing: Our ears pick up different sounds as we sit quietly and listen.

Sense of taste and smell: Our nose helps to smell things, and our tongue helps to taste different food. Our nose and tongue work together so we can enjoy the food that we eat.

Sense of touch: Our skin gives us the sense of touch. It tells us what we are feeling as we touch something. The skin is the biggest organ in the human body.

Tick (✓)

Do you	Yes	No
touch your eyes with dirty hands?	☐	☐
wash your hands often?	☐	☐
cut your nails regularly?	☐	☐
strain your eyes by watching too much TV?	☐	☐
eat healthy food?	☐	☐
keep your nose clean?	☐	☐

Learn More

Remember the sound of musical instruments, of rain, of flowing water or of any bird or animal.
Which of these sounds makes you happy?

Self Check

- Each one of us is unique. ☐
- The organs inside our bodies are called internal organs; for example, heart, brain, lungs, stomach and small and large intestines. ☐
- Our skeleton is a framework of bones. ☐
- Posture is the way we sit, stand or walk. ☐
- We should maintain correct posture. ☐
- Our sense organs help us to see, hear, smell, taste and touch. ☐

____

____

Practice

1. Write the answers.

(a) This is a robot.  This is its control centre. 

What is yours? ______________________

(b) This is a helmet.  It protects the head. What protects your brain? ______________________

(c) This is a blender.  It churns food.

What churns the food you eat? ________________

(d) This is a bike pump.  It pumps air into tyres.

What pumps blood through your body? __________

2. Tick (✓) Yes for good posture and No for bad posture.

	Yes	No
(a) straight back	☐	☐
(b) drooping shoulders	☐	☐
(c) head held high	☐	☐
(d) straight shoulders	☐	☐
(e) bent back	☐	☐

3. Answer the following questions.

(a) What are internal organs? Name two internal organs.

(b) What is skeleton?

(c) Explain the functions of the different sense organs.

(d) Raman has difficulty in breathing. He may have a problem in his ________.

(i) lungs (ii) stomach (iii) liver (iv) kidneys

(e) Select the option that will complete the word in the given statement.

Our body has a framework of bones called S__ E __ E __ O __.

(i) W, D, N, L (ii) O, P, L, M

(iii) K, L, T, N (iv) K, L, E, N

4. Critical Thinking

(a) If you did not have bones in your body, how would it affect you? Discuss.

(b) How long is Bala's foot? _____cm

How long is your foot? _______ cm

Is your foot shorter than Bala's? __

5. Social Emotional Skills

What do you feel in your body when you are scared or nervous? What do you do to help yourself feel better? Discuss.

6. Creativity

If you could have any superpower in your body, what would it be? Discuss.

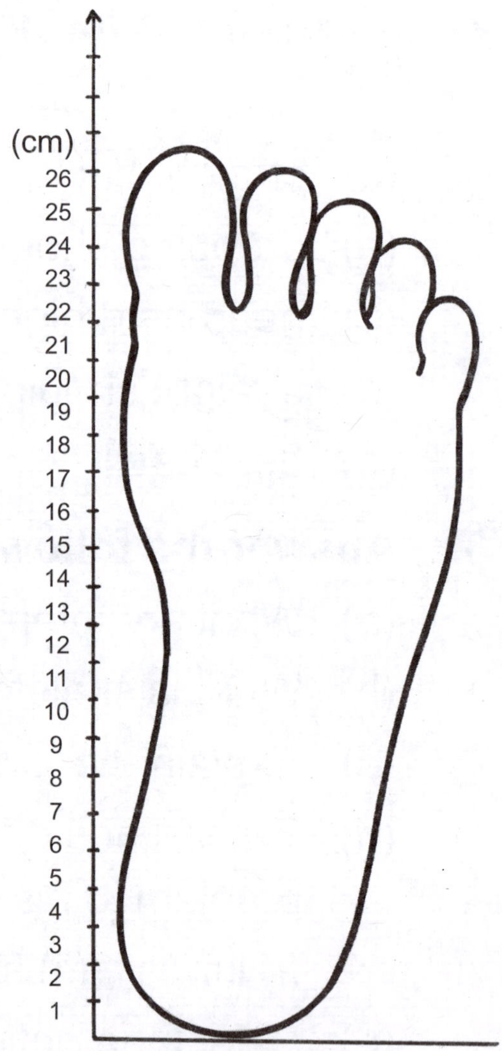

Bala's foot

2 My Family

Explore

What do your family members like to do in their free time?

	What they do
Your parents	
Your siblings	
Your grandparents	

Families have a lot of fun together. They help and care for each other. Families can be of different types:

- A family that has only parents and their children living together is known as a **nuclear family**.
- A family that is made up of grandparents, parents and their children living together is known as a **joint family**. Aunts and uncles and their families may also be a part of the joint family.

These are different kinds of families.

Sameera, her brother Vikram and their parents.

Amrinder and her parents.

Rehan, his mother and their dog.

Smita, her mother, her grandparents and their dog.

We celebrate special days, such as birthdays, anniversaries and festivals, with our families. We sometimes organise parties where we invite our friends and relatives. We also go for picnics and to shopping malls, cinemas and weddings with our family and friends.

Circle Time

Pets are an important part of some families. Do you have a pet or wish you had one? Have a discussion in class on what makes pets special.

Family Names

In most parts of India, all members of a family have a common family name or surname. The surname is usually written after a person's first name or given name. For example, Rohan Kapoor is a student of class two. His first name is Rohan and his family name (or surname) is Kapoor. Rohan's parents are Shiv and Lalita. They would write their full names as Shiv Kapoor and Lalita Kapoor.

In South India, however, families do not have common names. A person is identified by three names: the name of one's village, one's father's name and one's own name. Shankar Ravi's son, Sundaram, would be called Ravi Sundaram.

Sometimes, your parents may have different surnames. This is because some women change their surnames after they get married and some don't.

Nikita's parents lovingly call her 'Nikky' which is her nick name.

Learn More

Imagine you are celebrating your birthday party. Make a list of the people you would invite.

____

____

____

Self Check

- Family members help and care for each other. ☐
- A family can be nuclear or joint. ☐
- Family members have a common name or surname. ☐
- We celebrate special days with our family. ☐

Practice

1. **Fill in the blanks to complete the sentences.**
   (a) We live together as a ____________.
   (b) Rohan Kapoor's parents' surname is __________.
   (c) Some women change their ____________ after marriage.
   (d) We celebrate special days with our ____________.

2. **Put a (✓) for the correct statements and a (×) for the incorrect ones. Correct the incorrect statements.**
   (a) In a nuclear family, grandparents, parents and their children live together. ☐
   (b) A family gives us love and care. ☐
   (c) The family name is never written with the first name. ☐
   (d) Family members should help each other. ☐

3. **Answer the following questions.**
   (a) What is the difference between a joint family and a nuclear family?
   (b) What is a surname?
   (c) Who are your uncles and aunts?
   (d) My friend Ajit Gupta's mother lovingly calls him 'Guddu'. Gupta is his ____ and Guddu is his ____.
      (i) middle name, nick name
      (ii) nick name, middle name

(iii) surname, nick name
(iv) surname, middle name

(e) Which family occasion does this picture show?

(i) birthday celebration
(ii) anniversary
(iii) wedding
(iv) house-warming party

4. Critical Thinking

(a) What would you do if you had to spend one day alone in your house? Discuss.

(b) Why do you think traditions are important for families? Discuss.

5. Social Emotional Skills

By what name do you call your grandparents? Describe what they look like. How do you spend time with them? Do they tell you stories or help with your school work? Discuss.

6. Creativity

Your parents help you in so many ways. On a chart paper, list the ways you can also help your parents, in groups.

3 My Home

Explore

Look at the pictures and write how Sandeep, Meera and Mahesh are helping at home.

_______________ _______________

_______________ _______________

The house we live in is called our home. We live with our family in our home. Our home gives us shelter and we feel safe in it. Our home protects us from heat, cold, animals and thieves.

What is the name of the place where you live? Find the pin code of your place.

People in different places live in different kinds of houses, depending on the climate and surroundings. But humans did not always live in houses.

Early humans (people who lived many thousands of years ago) lived in caves and forests. They ate fruits and roots of trees, and also hunted animals for food.

Features of a House

A good house has doors and windows that allow fresh air and sunlight to enter the rooms. Sunlight kills germs. If we do not get enough fresh air and sunlight in our rooms, we can fall sick.

Windows also provide us a view of our surroundings. Some houses have balconies on their upper floors as well.

A house must have good ventilation. The process by which stale and warm air goes out of the house to be replaced by fresh, cool air is called ventilation.

Ventilation is provided in our homes by windows and ventilators, which are openings near the ceiling.

While it is very important to let fresh air and sunlight enter our homes, we need to make sure that flies, insects and mosquitoes stay out. One easy way of doing this is to put wire nets on doors and windows. This keeps flies, insects and mosquitoes away but allows sunlight and fresh air to enter.

Learn More

Identify the types of houses shown below and differentiate between them.

Self Check

- Our home provides us with shelter and protects us. ☐
- Early men lived in caves and forests. ☐
- A good house must be ventilated, clean and well lit. ☐

Practice

1. Fill in the blanks to complete the sentences.

(a) ________________ are openings near the ceiling.

(b) If we do not get fresh air, we can fall ___________.

(c) Some houses have ___________ on their upper floors.

(d) ___________ on doors and windows help to keep flies, mosquitoes and insects out.

2. Tick (✓) the features that belong to a good house.

(a) clean, dust-free rooms ☐

(b) dirty and smelly toilets ☐

(c) proper disposal of household garbage ☐

(d) several windows to let in fresh air and sunlight ☐

(e) wire netting on doors and windows ☐

3. Answer the following questions.

(a) List any two features of a good house.

(b) How did early humans live?

(c) What is ventilation?

(d) Wire netting on doors keeps out__________ .

(i) air (ii) sunlight (iii) insects (iv) none of these

(e) A good house is____________ .

(i) well lit (ii) ventilated (iii) dirty (iv) both i and ii

4. Critical Thinking

(a) How was the life of early humans different from yours? Discuss.

(b) What do you think are important things you need when building a house? Discuss.

5. Social Emotional Skills

What are the things in your house that make you feel safe and happy? Discuss.

6. Creativity

Make a *toran* or any decorative piece for your home, using dried leaves.

4 My Neighbourhood

Explore

Find out details about any two of your neighbours.

Name	Address	Phone numbers

The area around our house is known as our neighbourhood. This can be a colony, a street or a group of streets. The people who live in our neighbourhood are our neighbours. We should help our neighbours when needed.

Places in the Neighbourhood

Most neighbourhoods have places that provide important services and things to the people who live there. Some of these are schools, markets, banks, malls, police stations, hospitals, fire stations, parks and garbage dumps.

School

Write these details about your school.

Name of your school ____________________

Address of your school ____________________

Name of the principal ____________________

Number of classrooms ____________________

A **school** is a place where we learn to read and write and gain knowledge about different things. We also learn languages and different subjects, such as mathematics and science. We make new friends and learn about new cultures, different people and their religions.

Exercise and play are very important activities in school. They sharpen our mind and keep us alert and fit. Many schools have playgrounds and games courts. Some schools have gymnasiums, auditoriums, skating rinks and even swimming pools.

We must follow all the rules of our school. We must wear neat and clean uniforms and be on our best behaviour in school. We must obey our teachers and be polite and friendly to our classmates.

Apart from our teachers and the principal, there are other people who help in running the school well. They are watchmen, helpers, sweepers, school gardeners and bus drivers. We must thank them for all that they do for us.

Circle Time

Discuss the ways in which your school helps you.

Market

A **market** has many shops that sell a variety of things. Most neighbourhoods have a market where people can get what they need for everyday use.

These are some of the shops you may find in the neighbourhood market.

A **bakery** sells breads, cakes, biscuits and buns.

A **milk vendor** sells milk, butter, paneer and ice-cream.

A **greengrocer** sells fruits and vegetables.

A **grocery shop** sells things we need daily, such as spices, soap, shampoo, pulses and eggs.

Some neighbourhoods also have chemist shops which sell medicines. There may also be stationery shops where we can buy pens, pencils, erasers and notebooks.

Bank

A **bank** is a place where people keep money in a savings account. We go to a bank to withdraw or deposit money. We can also keep our valuables safe in a bank.

bank

Go to an ATM with your parents. Find out its use. What is the full form of ATM?

Hospital

Some neighbourhoods also have a **hospital** where doctors and nurses take care of people who are unwell.

Other neighbourhoods, that do not have a hospital, might have a dispensary or a doctor's clinic. A clinic is much smaller than a hospital and only a few doctors are available there.

hospital

Factastic!

If there is an emergency, we can dial 100 on the telephone to call the police. To call an ambulance, we dial 102.

Fire Station

If a fire breaks out in the neighbourhood, we dial 101 to call the fire brigade. Firefighters, who work at the **fire station**, put out the fire with the help of fire engines.

fire engine

Park

One of the most well-liked places in a neighbourhood is the **park**. A park usually has many trees and an open ground covered with grass. It may have slides and swings for children. Some parks have walking and jogging tracks. People enjoy going to the park to exercise, play or get fresh air.

park

Police Station

The police officers at the **police station** keep the neighbourhood safe.

police station

Mall

A **shopping mall** or **shopping centre** is a building or a set of buildings where you can buy things. They usually have many shops. They can also have restaurants and a movie hall inside.

mall

Learn More

Look at the pictures of some community helpers who assist us in our daily lives. Paste appropriate stickers from the sticker page.

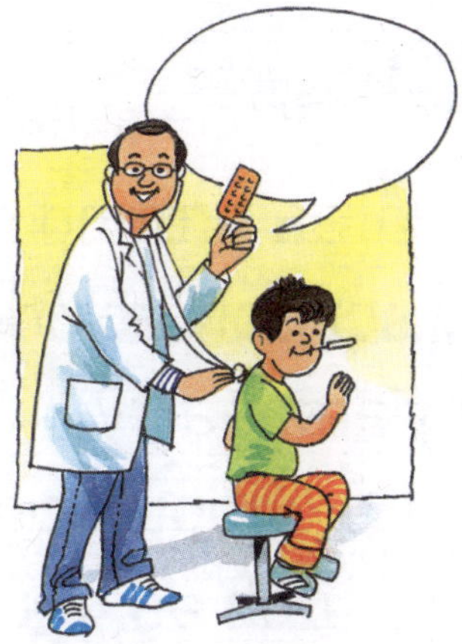

Self Check

- The area around our house is our neighbourhood. ☐
- Our school provides us with an education and builds our personality. ☐
- Our neighbourhood has places which make our life easy, such as, a market, a mall, a cafe, a hospital, a park, a police station, a fire station and a bank. ☐
- We need to keep our neighbourhood clean. ☐

Practice

1. Match the items in Column A with the places where we can buy them in Column B.

A		B
(a) medicines	•	• milk vendor's shop
(b) pens and pencils	•	• grocery shop
(c) milk and paneer	•	• chemist's shop
(d) soap and shampoo	•	• bakery
(e) biscuits and cakes	•	• stationery shop

2. Circle the correct words to complete the sentences.

(a) A (baker/police officer) works in a police station.

(b) In case of a medical emergency, we should call an (ambulance/bank).

(c) We go to the (greengrocer/hospital) when we are not feeling well.

(d) We can keep our jewellery and valuables safe at the (bank/hospital).

3. Answer the following questions.

(a) Name five kinds of shops you usually find in a neighbourhood market.

(b) What is a hospital? How does it help us?

(c) What are the things you find in a park?

(d) Four friends P, Q, R and S made four statements. Circle the INCORRECT statement.

(i) P — Today is my brother's birthday. I am going to a baker to order a cake.

(ii) Q — I want to eat paneer today, so I am going to the bank to get some paneer.

(iii) R — I have to buy some medicines prescribed by my doctor, so I am going to a chemist.

(iv) S — I want to make tomato soup, so I am going to a greengrocer to buy some tomatoes.

(e) Unscramble the letters. Now circle the name of the shop where you could buy notebooks, pencils and pens.

(i) AKBER (ii) TSATIONER

(iii) ARMFER (iv) EROGCR

4. **Critical Thinking**

(a) Why do you think neighbourhood have rules, like speed limit or keeping noise down at night? Discuss.

(b) How does living near other people help you and your family?

5. **Social Emotional Skills**

Different people do different kinds of work. Do you think we should respect all kinds of work? Discuss.

6. **Creativity**

If you could start a community garden in your neighbourhood, what plant and flowers would you grow? Draw and show it to your classmates.

5 Time to Celebrate

Explore

Identify the festivals shown in the following pictures. How do people celebrate these festivals? Discuss.

______________ ______________ ______________

Religious Festivals

Raksha Bandhan

Raksha Bandhan is celebrated on the last day of the month of *Shraavana* according to the Hindu calendar. On this day, sisters of all ages tie a *rakhi* around the wrists of their brothers. This festival celebrates the love between brothers and sisters.

Raksha Bandhan

Durga Puja

Durga Puja is a Hindu festival primarily celebrated by Bengalis. It is a five-day festival. During this festival, the idol of the goddess Durga is worshipped for four days and is immersed in water on the fifth day.

Durga Puja

Ganesh Chaturthi

an idol of Lord Ganesh

Ganesh Chaturthi is a Hindu festival where we worship the god Ganesh. It is a ten-day festival. During this festival, idols of Ganesh are worshipped privately in homes or publicly in elaborate *pandals*.

People distribute sweets, such as *modaks,* believed to be a favourite of the deity. The festival ends after ten days, when the idol is carried in a public procession with music and group chanting, and then immersed in a nearby water body.

This festival is celebrated especially in the states of Maharashtra, Goa, Telangana, Gujarat and Chhattisgarh.

National Festivals

Circle Time

How do you celebrate Independence Day in your society. Discuss.

National festivals are observed across the country as a symbol of national unity. The national flag is hoisted and we sing the national anthem on these days.

Independence Day

the Prime Minister addressing the nation from the Red Fort on Independence Day

In India, we celebrate Independence Day on 15 August every year. India gained freedom from the British on 15 August 1947. The Prime Minister hoists the national flag at the Red Fort in Delhi and addresses the nation. On this day, the national flag is hoisted across the country.

Republic Day

Republic Day parade

Republic Day is celebrated on 26 January every year. India became a republic on this day in 1950. It is the day when India's constitution came into force. The President of India takes the salute at the Republic Day parade in Delhi. The parade includes a march past by the army, navy and air force, performances by troupes of school children and floats representing the different states of India. The parade ends with a colourful fly-past by air force jets in a *tiranga* formation.

Gandhi Jayanti

Mahatma Gandhi

Mahatma Gandhi's birthday, 2 October, is celebrated as Gandhi Jayanti. Gandhiji played an important role in India's freedom struggle and is known as the 'Father of the Nation'.

Seasonal Festivals

Different parts of the country celebrate different seasonal festivals.

Basant Panchami

Basant Panchami marks the onset of spring. People wear yellow coloured clothes, offer yellow flowers to gods and apply yellow turmeric *tilak* on their foreheads to mark the onset of spring. Different regions celebrate Basant Panchami in different ways. In Bengal, people worship Goddess Saraswati on this day. In Punjab, people traditionally fly kites on this day.

Saraswati Puja

Pongal

Pongal is a three-day festival celebrating the harvest season in Tamil Nadu. It is celebrated in January every year. People worship the Sun God, the Rain God and the cow. On the third day, people prepare a special sweet dish, known as pongal rice, with jaggery and newly harvested rice.

preparation of pongal rice

Onam

snake boat race

Onam is celebrated in Kerala in August or September. King Mahabali is worshipped on this day. Decorated elephants are part of the processions that are taken out. Onam is famous for the snake boat race. The famous dance forms of Kerala are also on display during Onam.

Bihu

Bihu is celebrated in Assam in spring, autumn and winter. Bihu dance is a very important part of this festival. This festival celebrates the various stages of the farming process.

children performing Bihu dance

Lohri

Lohri is celebrated in January in North India, especially in Punjab. People light bonfires, sing folk songs and dance. This festival celebrates the end of winter and the harvesting of crops.

Lohri bonfire

Places of Worship

Every religion has different ways of praying to God. Do you pray? How?

All religions teach us to be good human beings, to be honest, kind, truthful and to help others in their time of need. Every religion has different places and ways of worship. Many pray to thank God for help and to ask for support. Some people pray in their homes, while others go to different places of worship to pray, especially on religious holidays. Some people may go to a place of worship every day, while others may go only once a week.

Temples

Hindus pray in temples. The priest is known as the *pujari* or *pandit*. People offer fruits and flowers as *prasad* to gods and goddesses, and light lamps and incense.

Birla Mandir in Delhi

Mosques

Muslims go to mosques to offer *namaaz* (prayers) five times a day. The *Koran* is the holy book of the Muslims.

Jama Masjid in Delhi

Gurdwaras

The Sikhs sing verses known as *gurbani* from their holy book, the *Guru Granth Sahib*, in *gurdwaras*. Guru Nanak Dev, the first of the ten *gurus*, was the founder of Sikhism.

Golden Temple in Amritsar

Churches

Christians go to church to offer prayers. The founder of Christianity was Jesus Christ. Christians go to the church every Sunday for a special prayer service. The *Bible* is the holy book of the Christians.

St. Francis Church in Kochi, the oldest church in India

Learn More

Go on a class visit to a temple, *gurdwara* or church and observe the different ways in which people pray.

Self Check

- India is a land of festivals. ☐
- Each religious community celebrates its own religious festivals such as, Raksha Bandhan, Durga Puja and Ganesh Chaturthi. ☐
- People also celebrate festivals from other communities. ☐
- National festivals are celebrated across the

country as a symbol of national unity.

- Different parts of our country celebrate different seasonal festivals like Pongal, Onam, Bihu and Lohri.
- Every religion has different ways of praying to God.

Practice

1. Complete the table.

Festival	Month/Season	State
Pongal		
		Kerala
		Assam
	January	
Basant Panchami		

2. Write T for true and F for false.

(a) Eid is celebrated on 25 December.

(b) Bihu is celebrated mainly in Punjab.

(c) The *Koran* is the holy book of the Hindus.

(d) Pongal is a three-day festival celebrated in Tamil Nadu.

3. Answer the following questions.

(a) How do people celebrate Durga Puja?

(b) What do sisters do on Raksha Bandhan?

(c) Name two harvest festivals that are celebrated in India.

(d) Ali is very happy today. He is wearing new clothes and is enjoying *meethi sewaiyan* made by his mother. Today is ________________ .

(i) Christmas (ii) Eid (iii) Holi (iv) Diwali

(e) Bihu is mainly celebrated in the state of _________ .

(i) Punjab (ii) Tamil Nadu

(iii) Kerala (iv) Assam

4. Critical Thinking

(a) Why is it important to celebrate festivals? Discuss.

(b) Do you think burning of crackers should be banned? Discuss.

5. Social Emotional Skills

How do you feel when a festival is coming up? What makes you excited about celebrating with your family and friends? Discuss.

6. Creativity

Collect pictures of different festivals celebrated in India and make a collage in groups.

6 Work and Play

Explore

Classify whether these games are played indoors or outdoors, and whether they are individual or team games. Tick the last box if you have played the game.

Game	Indoor	Outdoor	Individual	Team	Played
cricket	☐	☐	☐	☐	☐
ludo	☐	☐	☐	☐	☐
jigsaw puzzle	☐	☐	☐	☐	☐
badminton	☐	☐	☐	☐	☐
football	☐	☐	☐	☐	☐
carrom	☐	☐	☐	☐	☐
basketball	☐	☐	☐	☐	☐
table tennis	☐	☐	☐	☐	☐
hockey	☐	☐	☐	☐	☐
swimming	☐	☐	☐	☐	☐

We all need to eat nutritious food and keep our surroundings clean so that we can be healthy and strong. We must also play, exercise and get enough rest to remain fit.

Activities that refresh us and make us happy are known as **recreational** activities.

We all do different things in our free time. People play sports, read books and listen to music. Reading books is a very relaxing pastime. Some other popular hobbies are painting, sketching and collecting stamps.

Indoor games are those which we play in a covered area, such as a house or stadium.

Outdoor games are those which we play in a park or playground.

Individual games are those which we play alone or against others.

Team or **group games** are those where two or more people play together as a team.

Learn More

What are Paralympic Games? Do Indian athletes compete in Paralympic games? Find out.

Self Check

- We must eat nutritious food, play, exercise and get enough rest to stay healthy. ☐
- Recreational activities refresh us and make us happy. ☐
- Indoor games are played in covered areas and outdoor games are played in open playgrounds. ☐
- We can play games alone or in a group. ☐

____

____

Practice

1. Name the following

(a) A book you have read recently. ____________

(b) A TV programme you watch regularly. ________

(c) A game you like to play alone. ____________

(e) A game you like to play with your friends. ______

2. Correct the false statements.

(a) We eat junk food to keep healthy.

(b) Reading books is not a relaxing pastime.

(c) Cricket is an indoor game.

(d) We should watch TV for long hours.

3. **Answer the following questions.**

(a) What are outdoor games?

(b) Which is your favourite indoor game? Why?

(c) What are your hobbies?

(d) ________ is an activity that helps us to develop strong muscles.

(i) rope skipping (ii) painting

(iii) jogging (iv) both (i) and (iii)

(e) Circle the odd one.

(i) ludo (ii) badminton

(iii) cricket (iv) carrom

4. **Critical Thinking**

(a) Why is playing outdoor games better than watching TV? Discuss.

(b) Why is it important to have hobbies? Discuss.

5. **Social Emotional Skills**

Are some games meant only for girls or boys? Discuss.

6. **Creativity**

Do you like reading books?

Choose your favourite books.

Read them for at least 20 minutes every day for 20 days. Draw your favourite character.

7 Good Habits

Explore

Circle the items that we use to keep ourselves clean.

1.

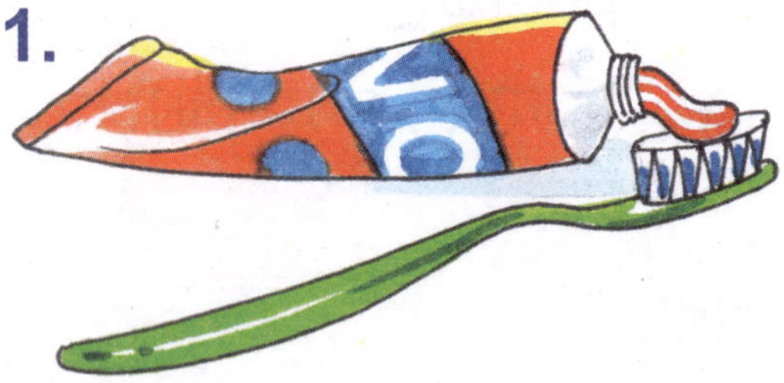

2.

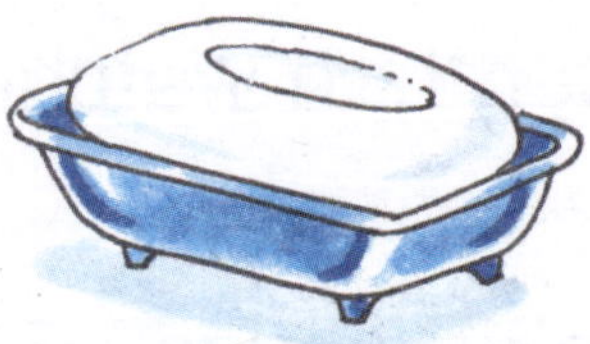

3.

4.

5.

6.

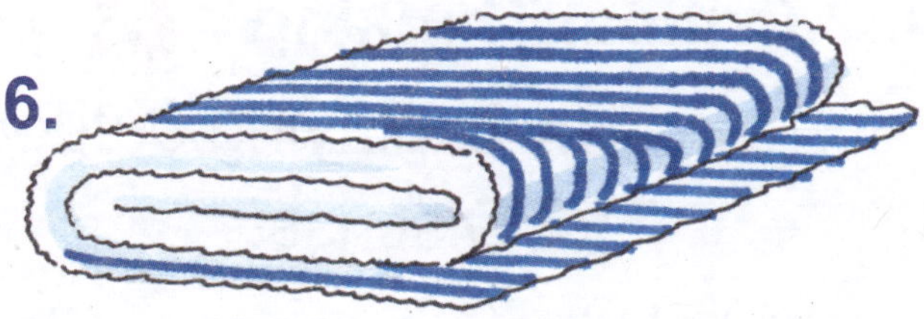

7.

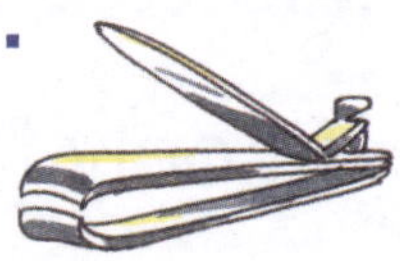

8.

9.

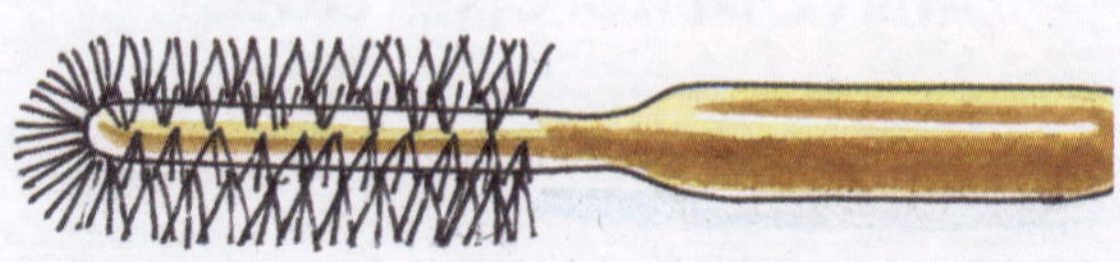

Keeping Clean

Keeping clean is very important to stay healthy. Cleanliness prevents diseases. Following are some of the things you need to do to keep yourself clean:

- Brush your teeth well every morning and every night.

- Take a bath with soap and water every day, and wipe yourself with a clean and dry towel.
- Always wear neat and clean clothes.
- Use a nail cutter to trim long nails. Do not bite your nails.
- Cover your mouth with a handkerchief when you yawn, cough or sneeze.

- Wash your hands well before you eat and after you go to the washroom.
- Keep your hair clean and neat.
- Keep your room tidy and clean.
- Keep your neighbourhood clean.

Importance of Exercise and Rest

yoga in school

Regular exercise keeps us fit. Walking, playing, running, yoga and dancing are various forms of exercise. We should exercise daily in fresh air. We also need to drink plenty of water. It helps to clean our body.

Getting enough rest is also important to keep ourselves healthy. We should sleep for at least 8 hours everyday.

How many hours do you sleep? ____________

Learn More

List the habits:

(a) you like in your friends.

____

____

(b) you like in yourself.

____

____

(c) you would like to change in yourself.

____

____

Self Check

- We need to keep ourselves clean to stay healthy. ☐
- We must keep our surroundings clean. ☐
- Cleanliness prevents diseases. ☐
- We need to sleep at least 8 hours a day. ☐
- We must drink plenty of water to clean our body. ☐

Practice

1. Match the columns. Column B lists what happens when you do not do the things listed in Column A.

A	B
brush teeth twice a day	body odour
bathe daily	tangled and dirty hair
wash hands before eating	germs on hands and an upset tummy
shampoo hair	spread germs
sneeze without a handkerchief	bad breath and cavities

2. **Write T for true and F for false.**

(a) We should not brush our teeth daily. ☐

(b) We should cover our mouth with handkerchiefs when we sneeze. ☐

(c) We should keep long nails. ☐

(d) We should not burp in public. ☐

3. **Answer the following questions.**

(a) When should we brush our teeth?

(b) What should we do while coughing or sneezing?

(c) How many hours should we sleep daily?

(d) Ramesh has a healthy diet, yet he falls ill frequently. What could be the reason for this?

(i) He does not comb his hair daily.

(ii) He does not trim his nails regularly.

(iii) He does not wash his hands properly before eating.

(iv) both (ii) and (iii)

(e) It is not a good habit to ______________ .

(i) throw waste in the dustbin

(ii) put out clean water for birds to drink

(iii) waste food by taking more food than needed

(iv) keep food covered

4. **Critical Thinking**

(a) Can we change our habits? How? Discuss.

(b) Why is it important to sleep early? Discuss.

5. **Social Emotional Skills**

(a) When you feel upset or angry, what are some healthy ways you can cope with those feelings? Discuss.

(b) Should we make a time table for our daily activities? Discuss.

6. **Creativity**

Just like you follow a time table in school, you can do a lot more if you have a time table for all the other things you do. Now fill up the following table to plan your week.

Days	Study time (h/min)	Screen time (h/min)	Reading (h/min)	Playing (h/min)
Sunday				
Monday				
Tuesday				
Wednesday				
Thursday				
Friday				
Saturday				

8 Food

Explore

Match the food to the plate.

We need food to live. The food that we eat provides us with the energy to study, play and remain active. It helps us to grow and remain healthy and strong.

We get our food from different plants and animals.

Types of Food

We must eat different types of food. Each type of food plays a different role in our body.

Energy-giving Food

Food which gives us energy to work, play and remain active is called energy-giving food. Rice, potatoes and bread are examples of energy-giving food. This category also includes cheese, butter, ghee and oil.

Protective Food

Fruits, vegetables and nuts help us to remain fit and prevent us from falling ill. They help us fight diseases and keep us healthy. They are examples of protective food.

Body-building Food

Fish, milk, eggs, meats and nuts help the body to grow and build muscle strength. They are examples of body-building food.

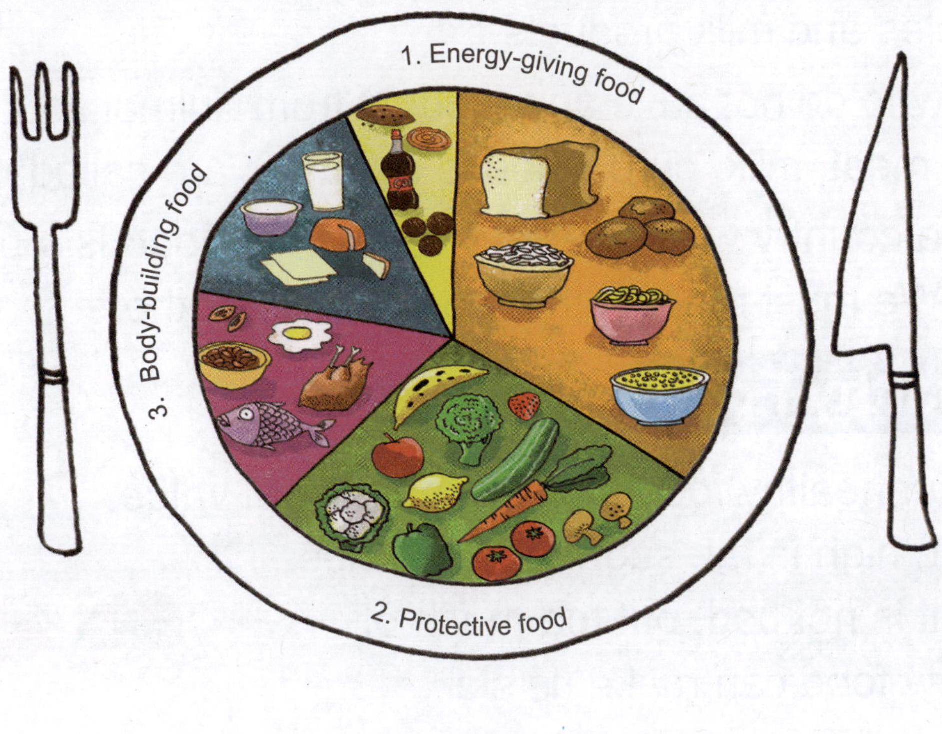

Balanced Diet

A diet which has a variety of food from all the food groups, in the required amounts, is called a balanced diet. A balanced diet provides us with energy, helps us grow properly and keeps us healthy and strong.

We also must drink plenty of water. Water has several important functions in the body. Three-fourths of our body is made up of water. Water helps maintain the body's temperature. It helps the nutrients travel to all parts of the body. Water is also good for the skin and helps the body to process food more efficiently.

Food Choices

Some people eat eggs, meat, fish and chicken. They are called **non-vegetarians.**

People who do not eat meat, fish and chicken are called **vegetarians**. Their diet consists of fruits, cereals, pulses, vegetables and milk products

People who do not have any product from animal sources, such as meat, milk, curd, cheese or butter, are called **vegans**.

India is a country with diverse food habits. Food is a personal choice. We must respect the food habits of others.

Unhealthy Food

Junk or unhealthy food is low in nutritional value. It is often high in fat, sugar and calories. A little bit is not bad, but too much of unhealthy food can make us sick.

Learn More

Tick the good food habits.

- Eat 'street food' often. ☐
- Eat fresh fruits and vegetables. ☐
- Wash fruits and vegetables well before eating them. ☐
- Eat at different times every day. ☐
- Eat alone in front of the TV. ☐
- Eat only one food group every week. ☐
- Store cooked food outside the refrigerator. ☐
- Chew food properly. ☐
- Waste food. ☐
- Talk while eating. ☐
- Wash hands before eating. ☐
- Sit at the dining table to eat meals. ☐
- Never wash fruits and vegetables with water. ☐
- Cook food in clean vessels. ☐
- Overcook or burn food. ☐

Self Check

- Food gives us energy and helps us to stay healthy.
- There are three kinds of food: energy-giving food, body-building food and protective food.
- People have different food choices.
- A balanced diet includes food from all food groups.
- We must eat a balanced diet to keep ourselves healthy.

Practice

1. Classify the food items below as healthy or junk food. Write H for healthy and J for junk in the boxes.

2. **Write T for true and F for false.**

(a) Potatoes, rice, bread and *chapattis* are body-building foods. ☐

(b) We need only air and water to be healthy and strong. ☐

(c) Fruits, vegetables and nuts protect us from diseases. ☐

(d) We must only eat uncovered foods. ☐

(e) We must eat different kinds of foods in the correct quantity. ☐

3. **Answer the following questions.**

(a) What are the different kinds of food?

(b) What is a balanced diet? How is it important for us?

(c) Give two examples of each.

(i) energy-giving food: __________ __________

(ii) body-building food: __________ __________

(iii) protective food: __________ __________

(d) Misha dislikes milk and milk products and refuses to have them. Her meals are mainly made up of rice, pulses and fish. This diet will eventually result in weak __________ .

(i) muscles (ii) bones

(iii) teeth (iv) both (ii) and (iii)

(e) We should not skip this meal because the body requires it the most as there is a long gap after the last meal. What is this meal?

(i) evening snacks (ii) dinner

(iii) lunch (iv) breakfast

4. Critical Thinking

(a) Can we cook food without heat? Discuss.

(b) How can we avoid wastage of food? Discuss.

5. Social Emotional Skills

How do you feel after you eat healthy food, like fruits and vegetables? What about after eating junk food? How do those food affect your energy and mood?

6. Creativity

Make a diet chart for yourself (breakfast, lunch and dinner) for one day. Make sure you include food from all three categories: energy-giving, body-building and protective food.

Meal	Food items
Breakfast	
Lunch	
Dinner	

9 Clothes

Explore

Just like you wear a uniform to school, some people wear special clothes according to the work they do. Identify these people in uniform.

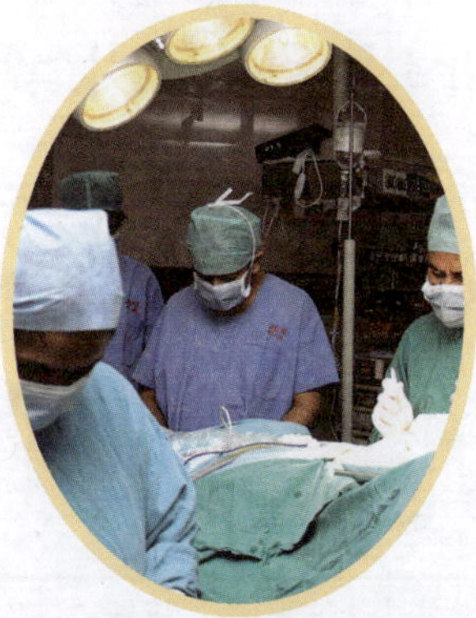

______________ ______________ ______________

Early humans did not wear clothes. At some point, they started using leaves to cover themselves. Later, they used the skins and furs of animals they killed to protect their bodies from extreme heat and cold.

We wear clothes to cover our bodies and to protect ourselves from heat, cold, wind, rain, dust and insects. We also wear clothes to look smart.

We must change our clothes every day. People wear different types of clothes in different seasons, in different countries and according to how they spend their day.

Types of Clothing

Our clothes change according to the season. In **summer**, we wear clothes that help us stay cool. We wear light clothes made of cotton, which is obtained from the cotton plant. Cotton clothes absorb sweat and keep us cool.

During **winter**, we need to wear clothes that keep us warm. Woollen garments help to keep us warm. We get wool from sheep, lambs, camels and even rabbits. Another material that is used in winters is silk.

Factastic!

In the rainy season, we wear waterproof clothing to protect ourselves from the rain. These clothes are usually made of plastic or rubber.

Natural and Man-made Fibres

Cotton, silk and wool are **natural fibres**. These are obtained from natural sources like plants and animals.

Nylon and rayon are examples of **man-made fibres**, which are prepared with different chemicals. Man-made fibres are more durable and stronger than natural fibres.

We sometimes use jackets, coats and caps made of leather to keep ourselves warm. Leather is also used to make shoes, belts and bags. We get leather from the skin of cows, goats, buffaloes and snakes.

People from different countries wear different kinds of clothes.

Colour the different clothes.

Baju Kurung and Baju Melayu from Malaysia

Kilt from Scotland

Kimono from Japan

Thobe and Abaya from Saudi Arabia

Learn More

How do we get silk fabric? Find out where we get silk from.

Self Check

- Clothes cover our body and protect us from extreme weather conditions. ☐
- We wear clothes according to different seasons, occasions and places. ☐
- Natural fibres are obtained from natural sources. ☐
- Man-made fibres are prepared by humans. ☐

____

____

Practice

1. Identify the materials from which the following items of clothing are made.

(a) W _ _ l 

(c) c _ t _ _ _ 

(b) r _ _ _ _ _ r 

(d) l _ _ t _ _ _ 

2. Write T for true and F for false.
Correct the false statements.

(a) We wear clothes to cover our body. ☐

(b) We wear the same clothes in different seasons. ☐

(c) People in different countries wear the same clothes. ☐

(d) We wear waterproof clothes in summer. ☐

3. Answer the following questions.

(a) What did early humans use to cover themselves?

(b) What kind of clothes do we wear during the rainy season?

(c) Where do we get wool from?

(d) We get _________ fibre from the animal shown here.

(i) woollen (ii) cotton

(iii) silk (iv) nylon

(e) Sheena's grandmother is making a scarf from wool, as shown in the picture. What is this method called?

(i) weaving (ii) spinning

(iii) knitting (iv) none of these

4. Critical Thinking

(a) Why do people in different countries wear different clothes? Discuss.

b) What do you think clothes will look like in thre future? Discuss.

5. Social Emotional Skills

Have you ever shared clothes with a sibling or a friend? How did that make you feel?

6. Creativity

Bring small cuttings of different types of fabric (cotton, wool, silk and nylon). Make a collage on a chart paper in groups.

10 Shelter

Explore

Unscramble the words to find the correct name of the animal home.

dog

klnnee ____________

pig

yst ____________

sheep

mfar ____________

cow

hsde ____________

horse

btlaes ____________

lion

ecva ____________

Early humans roamed the land to find food. They did not have permanent homes. They lived in caves.

As humans learnt to cultivate food crops and domesticate animals, permanent shelters became more common. The shelters that they built depended on the materials that were available and the climate of the place where they lived. Today, humans live in many different kinds of houses.

Types of Houses

People living in towns and cities make houses using bricks, stones, cement and steel. Such houses are strong and last for several years. They are known as **permanent** houses or *pucca* houses. These houses cannot be moved from one place to another.

Some people live in huts. Huts are made of straw and mud. These are known as **temporary** or *kuccha* houses.

kuccha houses

Factastic!

Many people in Kashmir live in houseboats known as *shikaras*. Nowadays, houseboats are also used for leisure trips.

Log huts are made of logs. These houses are found in the hills.

In places which receive a lot of rain, houses are built on wooden stilts.

stilt house

People who do not live in one place, but move from one place to another, are known as **nomads**. They live in tents and caravans.

A tent is a temporary shelter made up of fabric or other material, attached to a frame of poles or to a supporting rope.

tent

A caravan is a vehicle that is equipped for living and can be dragged by animals. Gypsies and *banjaras* live in caravans.

caravan

Igloo

Houses in cold places are made with blocks of ice. These are called igloos. Eskimos live in igloos and stay warm.

igloos

Find the places where Igloos are normally found.

Learn More

Are igloos, tents and skyscrapers suitable for all weather conditions? Fill up the table accordingly.

× means not suitable for that weather; ✓ means suitable.

	Hot/Sunny	Cold	Windy	Rainy	Snowy

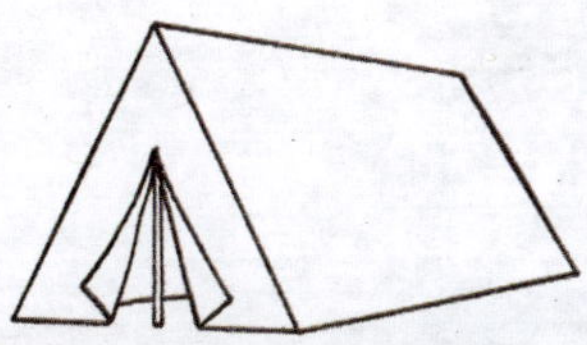					

Self Check

- Our house protects us and keeps us safe. ☐
- Permanent/*pucca* houses are made of cement, bricks, wood, glass and iron. ☐
- Temporary/*kuccha* houses are made

of mud, straw, wood and leaves. ☐

- Some people live in special houses like houseboats, igloos, tents, caravans, etc. ☐

____

____

Practice

1. Identify the homes below and write one line about each.

____

____

____

____

2. Circle the correct words to complete the sentences.

(a) A temporary house is made of (mud and straw/ bricks and cement).

(b) Houses are built on (straw/stilts) in places where it rains a lot.

(c) A house protects us from (postmen/thieves).

(d) A log house is made of (wooden logs/bricks).

(e) Caravans and tents are examples of (permanent/ temporary) houses.

3. **Answer the following questions.**

(a) What is the importance of a house?

(b) Write the differences between permanent and temporary houses.

(c) What is a *shikara*?

(d) Ashok's house is built of wooden logs and has a sloping roof. Ashok probably lives in a place where ________.

(A) floods are common (B) heavy rainfall occurs

(C) snowfall occurs (D) the Earthquakes are common

(i) A and D (ii) A, B and C (iii) B and C (iv) C and D

(e) Look at the picture carefully and choose the correct option.

(i) There are many houses in one building.

(ii) Each houses is called a flat.

(iii) These houses are very strong and are made of bricks, cement and steel.

(iv) All of these

4. **Critical Thinking**

(a) Can you live in a tent? What problems would you face if you lived in such a house? Discuss.

(b) If you could live anywhere in the word, what kind of house would you want to live in? Why?

5. **Social Emotional Skills**

How do you feel when you have to share your room with others? What can you do to make sure they feel comfortable? Discuss.

6. **Creativity**

What all changes would you like to make in your house to make it environment friendly? List the features.

11 Communication and Transport

Explore

Which means of communication would you use to:

(a) wish your cousin in Turkey a happy birthday? ________

(b) invite your friend to a party? ________

(c) tell your grandmother, in a different city, about your birthday party? ________

(d) warn everyone about a lion that has escaped from the zoo? ________

(e) send your application for a competition, which closes today? ________

Communication

Sending or receiving information, ideas or news is known as communication. Communication can be between two people or between many people. There are many ways to communicate with each other across the world.

Factastic!

A long time ago, people used pigeons to carry messages from one place to another. The letter would be tied to a pigeon's feet, and it would fly across long distances to deliver it to people in different towns and cities.

Letters

After we drop letters into a post box, a postman collects them and takes them to the post office.

At the post office, letters are sorted according to the different places to which they need to be delivered.

The sorted letters are sent to other places by bus, train or aeroplane.

As the letters reach the post office in the other city or town, they are again sorted.

The postman delivers these letters to the address written on them.

Telephone

telephone

A telephone enables us to talk to someone who lives far away from us. Nowadays, we also use cellular mobile phones, which can be used even while we are travelling.

> **Factastic!**
>
> The first cellular phone was invented by Dr Martin Cooper in 1973. The phone was known as the Motorola Dyna TAC 8000X.

Fax Machine

A fax machine sends and receives printed messages within a few seconds. Every fax machine has a specific number. The printed message is inserted into the sender's machine and the number of the receiver is dialled. The receiver's machine prints a copy of the original message within a few seconds.

Mass Communication

radio

Mass communication means to convey a message to many people at the same time. Newspapers, magazines, radio and TV are used for mass communication. A radio station sends messages through the air. These signals are picked up by radio sets. People can listen to the news, music programmes, audio plays, debates and discussions on the radio. Important information and alerts can also be transmitted over the radio.

The television (TV) is perhaps the most popular means of communication. Many different programmes are available on TV, such as news, cartoons, informative documentaries, live telecasts and entertainment programmes.

television

Satellites are used to send and receive messages from different parts of the world. Many countries have sent satellites into space for this purpose.

Internet

The Internet is one of the latest means of communication. We can send and receive messages and mails on the Internet.

Internet

We can also use it to find and exchange information on many different subjects. To use the Internet, we need a computer or a mobile device and an internet connection.

How do your parents go to work? Discuss.

Transportation

Transportation is the movement of people and goods from one place to another. Early humans did not have any means of transport. To get from one place to another, they had to walk or run. Later, when humans started domesticating animals, they used animals such as oxen and horses to carry heavy loads.

They also learnt to build boats to transport themselves and their goods from one place to another by river. Thereafter, once the wheel was invented, wheeled transport made it possible for humans to travel greater distances and transport heavier loads than before. Today, we travel from one place to another using air, land and water transport.

Fuels

Modern vehicles need fuel in order to move. Petrol, diesel, coal, compressed natural gas (CNG) and electricity are examples of fuels we use to make our vehicles run.

CNG cylinder

Learn More

Have you ever experienced a traffic jam? What are the possible causes of a traffic jam? Find out.

Self Check

- Means of communication keep us connected to people. ☐
- Letters, e-mail, fax and mobiles are used for communication. ☐
- Radio, TV and newspaper are means of mass communication. ☐
- There are three types of transport: land, water and air. ☐

- Fuel, such as petrol, diesel or CNG, is required to run different vehicles. ☐

Practice

1. Provide one-word answers for the following.

(a) Name one means of water transport.

(b) Name one very popular means of communication.

(c) Name one means of air transport.

(d) Name one means of land transport that does not require fuel.

(e) Name one means of communication used a long time ago.

2. Write T for true and F for false statements. Correct the false statements.

(a) Letters are used for sending urgent messages. ☐

(b) Computers are not a means of communication. ☐

(c) Every fax machine has a specific number. ☐

(d) Early humans did not have any means of transport. ☐

3. Answer the following questions.

(a) What is transport? Name the different means of transport you use.

(b) What factors does our choice of transport depend on?

(c) What is communication? What are the different kinds of communication?

(d) Sonu made four pairs, each with two of the same type of transport. However, one of those pairs is incorrect. Identify the INCORRECT one.

(i) helicopter, aeroplane (ii) car, submarine

(iii) sailboat, steamship (iv) truck, bus

(e) Nowadays, people sitting in a far off place can talk to and see each other with the help of telecommunication and computers. This is done through __________ .

(i) e-mail (ii) video conferencing

(iii) news telecast (iv) fax

4. Critical Thinking

(a) How do you watch a live telecast of a cricket match happening in Australia? Discuss.

(b) What would happen if internet connection of the entire world stopped working for a day? Discuss.

5. Social Emotional Skills

Why is it important to be patient when waiting for transportation, like a bus, a train or a flight? Discuss.

6. Creativity

If you could design an eco-friendly transport, what features would it have? Where would it take people? How would it look like?

12 Directions and Maps

Explore

Give the turtle directions to reach the treasure. Draw arrows along the dotted path.

up = ↑ , left = ← , right = → down = ↓

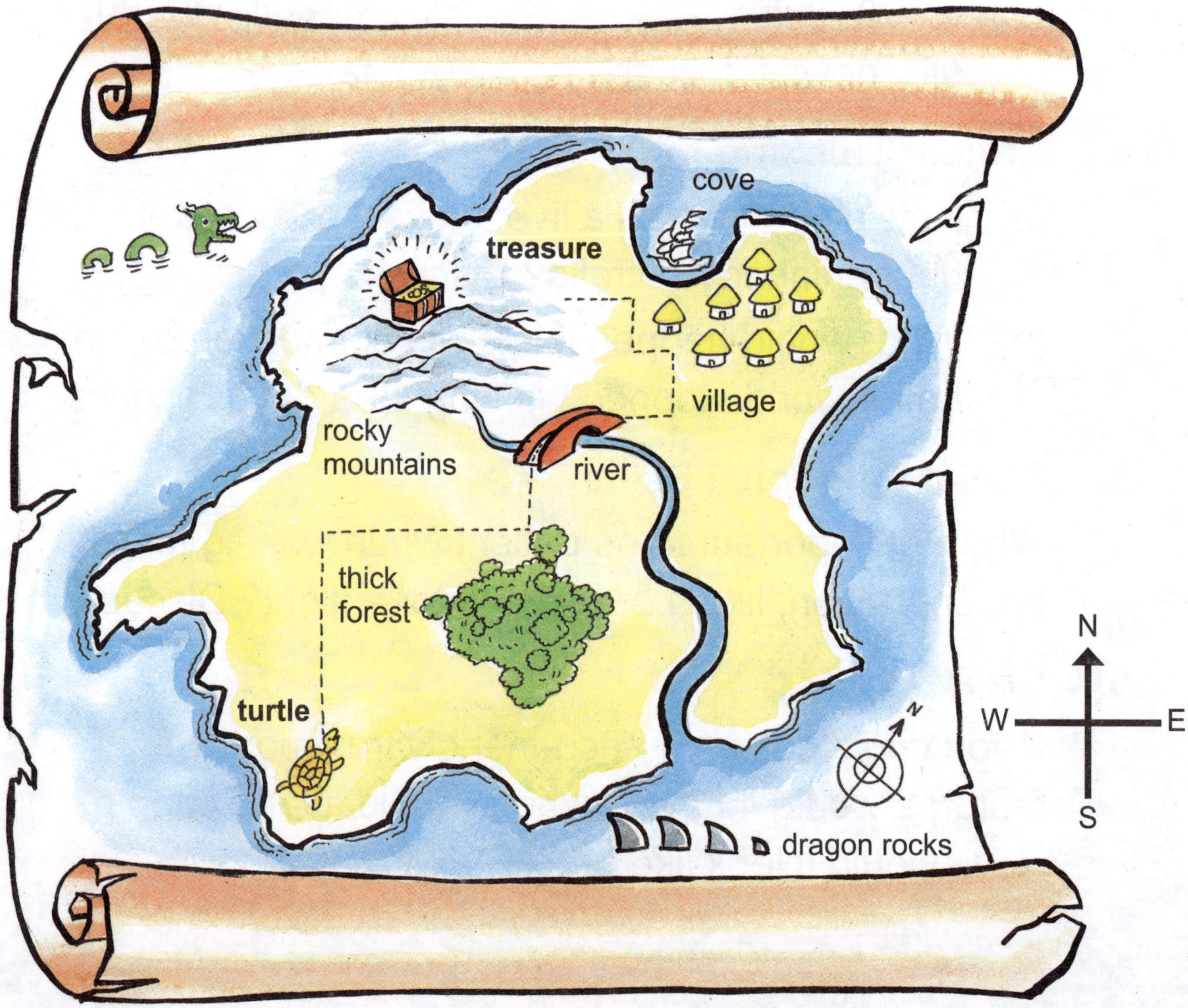

If you stand straight, you will find that you can move your arm on six sides: front, back, up, down, right and left.

up-down

front-behind

right-left

Directions

There are different ways to get to the same place. To go somewhere, we need to know the directions to that place.

When we say that a place is to the left or to the right, or it is up the street or down the street, we are giving directions. Without them, we can get lost.

The four main directions are North, South, East and West.

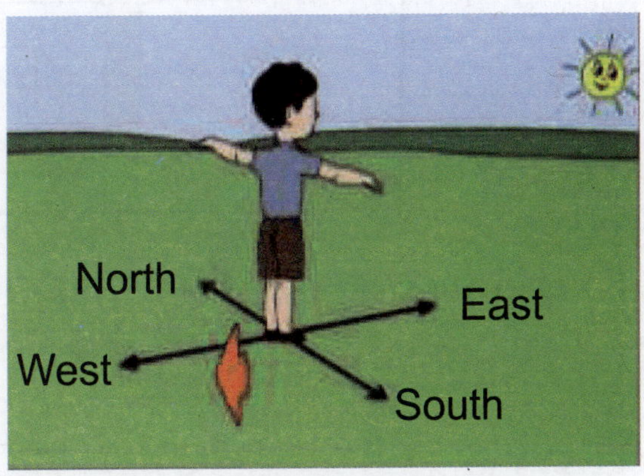

The Sun rises in the East and sets in the West. If you stand facing the Sun in the morning, your front is towards the East and back points to the West. Your left hand points to the North and right hand points to the South.

A compass helps us identify directions. The needle of a compass always points to the North. If you do not have a compass, you can tell the direction by seeing where the Sun rises and sets or by checking the position of the North Star at night.

Maps

A map is a drawing that shows us the location of a place, a neighbourhood or a city. We use it to find our way. There are different types of maps.

Rani lives in Fun City. Her house is on Green Avenue. Find her house. Choose the correct option and fill in the blanks.

To get to the park, Rani goes _____. (West, East, South)

The mall is to the _____ of Rani's house. (North, South, West)

The post office is to the _____ of the mall. (South, East, West)

To go to school, Rani goes _____. (South, North, East)

Traffic Signs

Traffic signs or road signs are signs we see on the roadsides. They provide information to all those who use the roads.

 Cycle crossing

 Pedestrian crossing

 School ahead

 Men at work

 Roundabout

 No parking

 No stopping or standing

 Horn prohibited

Learn More

What is a traffic park? Find out the nearest traffic park.

Self Check

- There are four main directions: North, South, East and West. ☐
- We can use a compass to identify directions. ☐
- Maps show us the location of a place. ☐

____

____

Practice

1. **Stick the appropriate traffic sign stickers in the scene on the next page. The stickers are provided on the sticker page.**

Zebra cro
Men at work
Only fo
Park

T - Junction
Hospital
No horn
Fire station
Trafic island
No parking
school
School ahead
lists

2. **Write T for true and F for false statements. Correct the false statements.**

(a) There are five main directions. ☐

(b) Maps are not useful. ☐

(c) All maps are of the same type. ☐

(d) The Sun sets in the West. ☐

3. **Answer the following questions.**

(a) How are maps useful?

(b) Name the four main directions.

(c) Where can you see a collection of maps?

(d) The road sign shown here means that a/an _________ is nearby.

(i) hospital (ii) school

(iii) bus stop (iv) airport

(e) The traffic police officer is signalling to stop vehicles approaching from _________ .

(i) behind (ii) the front

(iii) the left and right sides (iv) both (i) and (ii)

4. **Critical Thinking**

(a) How would it affect the drivers if pedestrians do not follow traffic signs? Discuss.

(b) Why is it important to know how to give directions? Discuss.

5. **Social Emotional Skills**

Why is it important to listen carefully when someone gives you directions? How can you show you are listening?

6. **Creativity**

Draw a map of the way from your classroom to the library in your school, in groups.

13 Safety

Explore

The picture below shows certain actions that are dangerous. Circle these actions with a red pencil and discuss.

____

____

____

Safety

To stay away from danger, we must follow safety rules while travelling, at home and outside.

Safety on the road

You must already be aware of the safety tips to be observed on the road. Tick (✓) the correct boxes.

	Yes	No
Observe all traffic signals	☐	☐
Walk on the pavement	☐	☐
Run and cross the road	☐	☐
Play on the road	☐	☐
Use the zebra crossing to cross the road	☐	☐
Look left, then right and then left again before crossing the road	☐	☐
Wear a helmet when riding a bike	☐	☐
Wear a seat belt while travelling by car	☐	☐
Flash bright lights at oncoming traffic	☐	☐
Obey the traffic police	☐	☐
Ride a bicycle on busy roads	☐	☐

Safety on the bus

It is very important to observe safety rules while travelling by bus.

Tick (✓) the correct boxes.

	Yes	No
Run and get onto the bus	☐	☐
Push and shove your friends	☐	☐
Never get onto a moving bus	☐	☐
Wait for your turn to get onto the bus	☐	☐
Lean out of the window	☐	☐
Stick your hand out of a moving bus	☐	☐

Safety in the car

Do you observe safety rules while travelling by car?

Tick (✓) the correct boxes.

	Yes	No
Sit in the rear seat of the car	☐	☐
Disturb the driver	☐	☐
Keep the doors locked in a moving car	☐	☐
Play with the knobs of windows	☐	☐
Allow the driver to talk on the mobile phone	☐	☐
Never jump a red light	☐	☐
Ask the driver to go over the speed limit	☐	☐
Wear a seat belt	☐	☐
Play with the locks of doors	☐	☐
Put your head or hand outside the window of a moving car	☐	☐
Jump into a moving car	☐	☐

Safety in the swimming pool

Splashing in the swimming pool with friends is great fun. But some important safety rules need to be followed in the swimming pool.

Tick (✓) the correct boxes.

	Yes	No
Never swim alone in the pool	☐	☐
Use a swimming tube or floaters	☐	☐
Go to the deep end without the lifeguard on duty	☐	☐
Never run around the pool	☐	☐
Swim after eating a meal	☐	☐
Push friends into the pool	☐	☐
Disturb the other swimmers in the pool	☐	☐
Dive in the shallow end of the pool	☐	☐
Chew gum or eat while swimming	☐	☐

Safety at school

At school, teachers make sure we follow safety rules. Do you know all the rules to follow?

Tick (✓) the correct boxes.

	Yes	No
Push the other children	☐	☐
Lean across the railings	☐	☐
Jump down the stairs	☐	☐

Run in the corridors	☐	☐
Never touch electrical switches	☐	☐

Safety at home and at all times

Home is where we are safe and protected. Even so, we need to follow some important safety rules inside the house.

Tick (✓) the correct boxes.

	Yes	No
Touch electrical switches with wet hands	☐	☐
Play with electrical appliances	☐	☐
Let strangers into the house	☐	☐
Touch harmful chemicals and medicines	☐	☐
Walk down steps carefully	☐	☐

Play outdoor games inside the house ☐ ☐

Go near the gas stove ☐ ☐

Let people touch you where you are not comfortable ☐ ☐

Circle Time

How do you feel when your mother gives you a warm hug? How do you feel when a stranger tries to hug or touch you?

No Touch

There are many people who might want to hurt us. We must take care of ourselves and be careful of such people.
If somebody touches us in a way that makes us uncomfortable, hurts us or gives us the 'uh-oh' feeling, we must say 'no' and move away, and immediately inform an adult whom we trust. This is for our own safety.

Learn More

What all safety measures does your mother take while working in the kitchen? Discuss with your mother.

Self Check

- We need to be aware to keep ourselves safe. ☐
- We can protect ourselves from danger by observing safety rules while at home and outside. ☐

Practice

1. Fill in the blanks to complete the sentences.

(a) We must not __________ on the roads.

(b) We must stand in a ________ and wait for our turn while boarding the bus.

(c) We must ________ quietly and not play in the car.

(d) We must not play with ________. It is very dangerous.

2. Write **T** for true and **F** for false statements. Correct the false statements.

(a) We should run and get into a moving bus. ☐

(b) We should disturb the driver while he is driving. ☐

(c) We should play with electrical appliances. ☐

(d) We should run and jump on the staircase. ☐

3. Answer the following questions.

(a) Write two safety rules that you should observe in school.

(b) Where should you cross the road?

(c) Write any two safety rules that you observe at home.

(d) We should never play with a ___________ .

(i) matchbox and matchsticks (ii) football

(iii) blade (iv) both (i) and (iii)

(e) Always walk on the _________ and cross the road at the __________, if there is one.

(i) footpath, zebra crossing

(ii) road, zebra crossing

(iii) footpath, subway

(iv) road, footpath

4. Critical Thinking

(a) Why is it important to be careful about sharing personal information online? Discuss.

(b) Why shouldn't we use mobile phones while driving? Discuss.

5. Social Emotional Skills

What will you do in case a stranger comes and starts talking to you? Discuss.

6. Creativity

Make posters on safety rules for the class, in groups and display in the class.

14 Living and Non-living Things

Explore

Stick the L sticker for living things and the NL sticker for non-living things, and colour the pictures. Stickers are provided on the sticker page.

Our environment includes everything around us: land, air, water, forests, animals, plants and people. Some of these are living things while others are not. All animals and plants are living things.

All living things must have certain features in order to be classified as living things.

Characteristics of Living Things

Living things grow: All living things grow. They go through various stages during their growth.

growth

movement

Living things move: All living things move. Some living things show external movement—they can move from place to place by walking, flying or swimming. Other living beings show restricted movements.

Living things breathe: All living things exchange gases with their environment. Living things breathe in oxygen and breathe out carbon dioxide. Plants need carbon dioxide for making food.

respiration

sweating

Living things remove waste: 'Excretion' is the removal of waste from the body. All living things need to remove waste from their bodies in the form of sweat, urine and faeces.

Living things eat: When living things eat, they gain energy, which is used in growth and movement. Animals eat plants or other animals, while plants make their own food using sunlight.

nutrition

Living things react to changes: Living things react to changes around them, such as touch, light, heat, cold and sound.

living things react

Living things reproduce: All living things produce young ones. Humans make babies, cats produce kittens and pigeons lay eggs. Plants also reproduce. Many make seeds which can germinate and grow into new plants.

reproduction

Non-living things do not display any of the characteristics of living things.

Non-living Things

Things like stones, glass, pencils, air and water are non-living things.

- Non-living things do not eat.
- Non-living things do not breathe or grow.
- Non-living things do not excrete or reproduce.

Learn More

Compare a chair and a cat. List their similarities and differences.

Self Check

- All plants and animals are living things.
- All living things grow, move, breathe, eat, remove waste, react to changes and reproduce.
- Non-living things do not eat, breathe, grow, excrete or reproduce.

Practice

1. Write L for living things and NL for non-living things.

2. Correct the following statements.

(a) We take in carbon dioxide.

(b) We do not need to remove waste from our body.

(c) Plants do not reproduce.

(d) Living things cannot grow.

3. Answer the following questions.

(a) Give the differences between living and non-living things.

(b) What is excretion?

(c) Which gases do animals take in and breathe out?

(d) All living things produce ________________ .

(i) light

(ii) young ones

(iii) food

(e) Which of the following statements suggest that a battery operated car is NOT a living thing?

(A) It takes up space.

(B) It is hard and shiny.

(C) It does not reproduce.

(D) It does not move on its own.

(i) A and B only (ii) A and C only

(iii) B and D only (iv) C and D only

4. **Critical Thinking**

(a) A car is a non-living thing, but it can move. Why?

(b) Why are plants living things while wood is non living thing? Discuss.

5. **Social Emotional Skills**

Living things react to changes. Do we have a choice in our reactions? Discuss.

6. **Creativity**

If you could create a new living thing, what would it look like and what special abilities would it have?

15 Plants

Explore

Observe the pictures and describe what is happening. Discuss with the rest of the class.

Observe the plants you see in your school and in your surroundings. Plants are of many sizes, shapes and colours. They can grow in very cold as well as very hot places.

Trees are big plants with strong stems called trunks. Gulmohar, banyan and mango are examples of trees.

banyan

apple

mango

Factastic!

Redwood trees are ancient giants, the tallest living beings on the Earth. They reach heights of up to 360 feet.

rose plant

Shrubs are small and bushy plants; for example, rose and hibiscus. They are also called **bushes**. Their height usually ranges from one to five metres.

Herbs have delicate stems and include plants such as mint, coriander and grass. Many herbs are edible and are used to flavour or season food.

coriander

grass

What herbs are used in your house? Find out.

____

____

dal garnished with coriander

Creepers are usually found growing along the surface of the soil as they have weak stems. Examples of creepers are pumpkin and watermelon.

pumpkin

Climbers are plants with very weak stems. They wrap themselves around other plants, rocks or man-made structures for support. For example, the money plant.

money plant

How a Seed Grows

Plants are living things. They cannot move about like animals, but they grow. They need sunlight, air, water and soil to grow. The length of time, from the beginning of the development to the death of a plant is known as its **lifespan**. Each plant goes through stages of growth and development that may include seed, sapling and mature plant.
Parts of a plant include roots, stems, leaves, flowers and fruits. Leaves make food for the plant, with the help of sunlight. The root of the plant grows under the soil and the shoot grows above the soil.

A seed is the part from which a new plant grows.

sapling: a young plant or even a tree

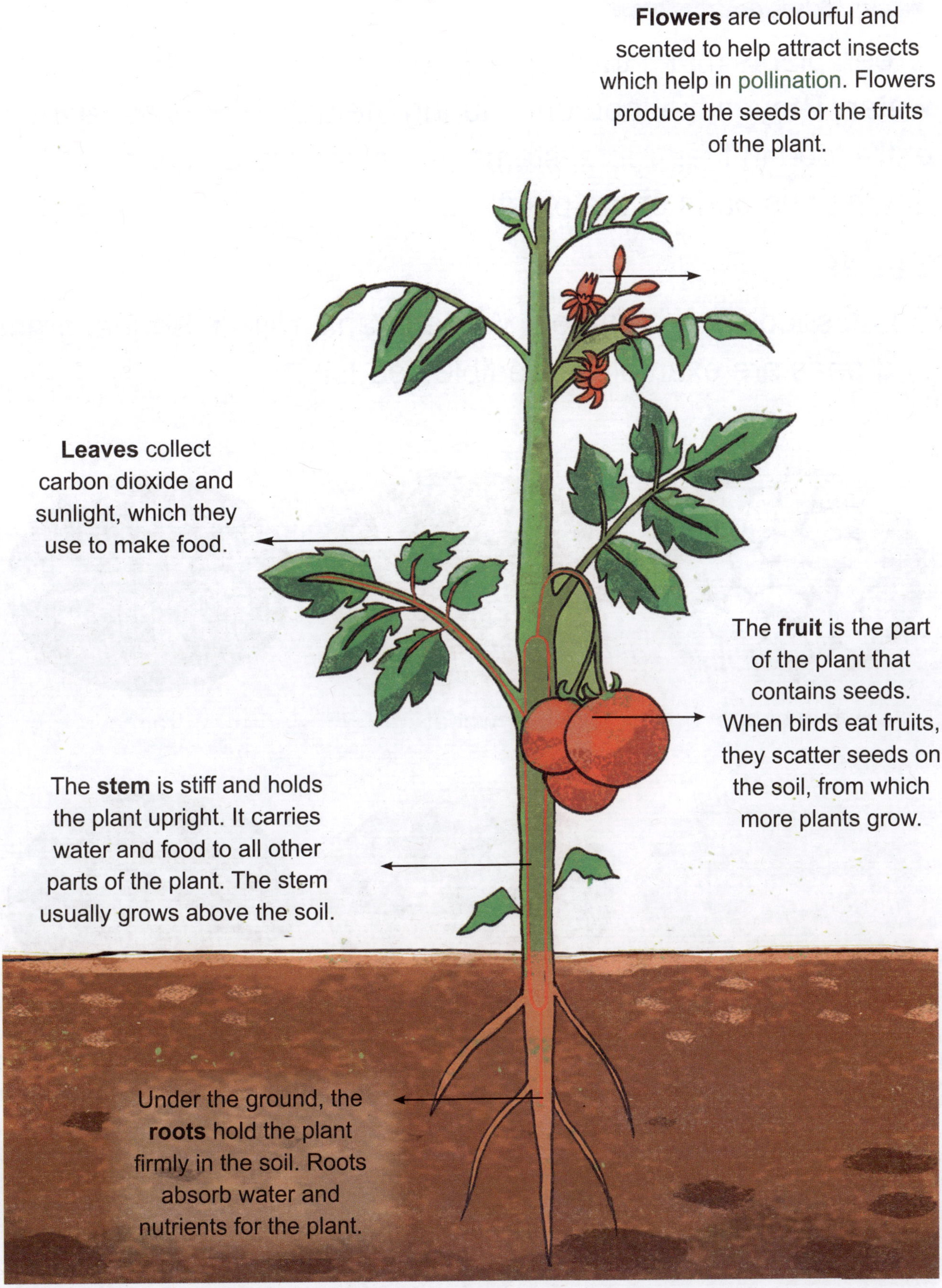
Flowers are colourful and scented to help attract insects which help in pollination. Flowers produce the seeds or the fruits of the plant.
Leaves collect carbon dioxide and sunlight, which they use to make food.
The **fruit** is the part of the plant that contains seeds. When birds eat fruits, they scatter seeds on the soil, from which more plants grow.
The **stem** is stiff and holds the plant upright. It carries water and food to all other parts of the plant. The stem usually grows above the soil.
Under the ground, the **roots** hold the plant firmly in the soil. Roots absorb water and nutrients for the plant.

Plants as Food

Green plants make their own food by using sunlight, air and water. They make food only during the day. Plants store the extra food in their roots, stems, fruits, leaves and seeds. We eat various parts of the plant.

Seeds

Some seeds can be eaten. White beans, rajma, Bengal gram and peas are examples of edible seeds.

white beans

wheat

rajma

rice

Bengal gram

peas

Stems

Stems usually grow above the ground, but some special stems, such as potato, grow under the ground. We eat stems such as sugarcane, potatoes, lotus stems and banana stems.

potato

sugarcane

Roots

Carrot, turnip and radish are edible roots.

carrot

turnip

radish

Leaves

Cabbage, spinach and lettuce are leaves that we eat.

cabbage

lettuce

spinach

Flowers

Cauliflower, as its name suggests, is a group of flower buds which can be eaten. Flowers of banana and drumsticks can also be eaten.

cauliflower

broccoli

Fruits

We eat pumpkins, tomatoes and ladies' fingers, which are actually fruits. However, most of these need to be cooked before they are ready for eating.

tomatoes

ladies' fingers

pumpkin

We also eat raw fruits such as oranges, pears and mangoes.

These fruits can be crushed and squeezed to make beverages. Other beverages like tea and coffee also come from plants.

Plants give us spices such as fennel and cumin. Spices add flavour to our food and are obtained from the seeds, roots and barks of different plants.

Other Uses of Plants

Plants keep our environment clean and green. Plants play a role in creating rain. We must not allow anyone to cut down trees; instead, we must grow more trees and plants.

cooking oil

paper

medicines

cotton

bamboo

perfumes

rubber

jute

wood

Some products we get from plants

Factastic!

Bamboo can grow up to three feet in a 24-hour period.

Learn More

Is mushroom a plant? Find out.

Self Check

- Humans and animals cannot survive without plants. ☐
- Plants provide us oxygen to breathe and food to eat. ☐
- Trees are big plants with strong stems, while herbs, creepers and climbers have soft stems. ☐
- The parts of a plant include roots, stem, leaves, flowers and fruits. We eat various parts of a plant. ☐

Practice

1. Label the plant parts in the picture.

2. **Take stickers of fruits, leaves, flowers and roots from the sticker page and place them in the correct box.**

Fruits	Leaf
Flowers	Roots

3. **Answer the following questions.**

(a) How are plants useful to us?

(b) What are the different parts of a plant that we can eat? Give examples.

(c) Differentiate between climbers and creepers.

(d) Plants give us food grains. Which of the following are examples of such grains?

(i) wheat and rice (ii) maize and barley

(iii) gram and pulses (iv) all of these

(e) The stem pulp of the plant shown here is used to make ___________.

(i) rubber (ii) gum

(iii) paper (iv) oil

4. **Critical Thinking**

(a) What will happen to a plant if we remove all the leaves from it? Discuss.

(b) Why are plants called 'lungs of the Earth'? Discuss.

5. **Social Emotional Skills**

Adopt a plant in your neighbourhood. Water it regularly and take care of it.

6. **Creativity**

What special powers would you like to give to a plant? How would it help people? Can you make it grow faster?

16 Animals

Explore

Colour in red the things that all animals do. Colour in green the things that only some animals do.

fly

grow

move

swim

speak

breathe

get rid of waste

lay eggs

jump

eat

reproduce

The Earth is the only known planet to have life on it. Animals are everywhere on the Earth, from the highest mountain to the bottom of the deepest ocean.

Polar bears live in very cold areas. Camels live in hot areas. the Earthworms live under the ground. Sharks live in the oceans.

Types of Animals

All animals need food to live. Animals can be classified into different categories based on the food they eat.

Some animals eat grass and leaves. Others eat fruits and nuts. Such animals are called **herbivores**.

deer

cow

squirrel

Carnivores are those animals that kill other animals and eat them, like lions, tigers, foxes and wolves. Carnivores have sharp teeth to tear flesh with.

lions

Omnivores are animals that eat both plants and animals. For example, pigs, rats, bears and humans.

bear

Factastic!

Vultures and hyenas eat the remains of dead animals. They are known as scavengers.

When animals die or are killed in large numbers, they become rare. They may then die out completely and become extinct. Some animals that are now extinct are dinosaurs and dodos.

Find out the names of some animals that are rarely found in India. Discuss with the rest of the class.

Uses of Animals

Some animals live on farms or in our backyards. They help us in many ways. These are known as **domestic** animals. For example, cats, dogs, sheep, goats, cows and horses. We can train some animals to work for us. Animals such as donkeys, horses, elephants and camels carry heavy loads for us.

sheep

Dogs help guard our homes. Dogs can also be trained to work as guides for the blind. They can also sniff out bombs and drugs, as they have a very keen sense of smell.

dog

We get milk from cows, buffaloes and even goats. Milk is used to make cheese, curd, ice cream and butter.

goat

The honey bee is an insect that is very helpful to us. It takes nectar from flowers and turns it into honey.

honey bee

Factastic!

We get wax from beehives. This wax is used to make candles, lipsticks and other things.

We get eggs from ducks and hens. Eggs are high in protein. Some of us also eat fish, chicken and mutton. They are rich in protein too.

hen

We get wool from sheep, which is used for making woollen clothes to keep us warm.

Factastic!

We get silk from the cocoons of silkworms.

Learn More

Match the birds and animals to the sounds they make.

lions •	• coo
pigs •	• chatter
dogs •	• roar
horses •	• moo
pigeons •	• bark
monkeys •	• grunt

cows •	• neigh
cats •	• buzz
bees •	• croak
frogs •	• mew

Self Check

- All animals need food to live. ☐
- Animals can be classified on the basis of the food they eat. ☐
- Herbivores, like deer and cows, eat only plants. ☐
- Carnivores, like tigers and lions, eat only flesh. ☐
- Omnivores eat both plants and animal flesh. ☐
- Animals provide us with milk, eggs and meat. ☐
- Animals are very useful to us. ☐

____

____

Practice

1. Fill in the blanks to complete the sentences.

(a) __________ is a domestic animal.

(b) We get __________ from hens and ducks.

(c) A __________ carries heavy loads for us.

(d) We get __________ from beehives.

(e) __________ eat the remains of dead animals.

2. Write T for true or F and false statements.

(a) All animals eat grass.

(b) Honey bees are not useful to us.

(c) We get silk from the silkworm.

(d) Foxes are domestic animals.

(e) Lions are omnivores.

3. Answer the following questions.

(a) What are carnivores? Give two examples.

(b) How are cows and buffaloes useful to us?

(c) How are vultures different from other birds?

(d) Ravi was asked to make four groups with three animals each, which are useful to humans in similar ways. But he made one mistake. Select the option with the mistake.

(i) donkey, camel, horse (ii) cow, goat, buffalo
(iii) hen, duck, goose (iv) elephant, mule, crocodile

(e) Select the option that correctly fills the blank in the given statement.

Moo, Moo, where are you?
Come to me. I will
give tasty _______ to you.

(i) leather (ii) egg (iii) milk (iv) oil

4. **Critical Thinking**

(a) Are animals also useful for plants? Discuss.

(b) If a polar bear lived in the desert, what problems might it face? Discuss.

5. **Social Emotional Skills**

If you see children throwing stones at a dog, what will you do? Discuss.

6. **Creativity**

If you could spend a day as any animal,which one would you like to choose and why? What kind of things would you do during your adventure?

17 Our Universe

Explore

Observe the night sky and share your experience with the rest of the class.

The Sun, the Moon and the stars are all heavenly bodies.

Stars

A star is a giant mass of very hot, glowing gas. Stars produce their own light and energy. There are so many stars in the sky that it is impossible for us to count them. New stars are born all the time. As stars age, they die. The Sun is the star nearest to the Earth.

The Sun

The Sun is a great ball of fire. It is the biggest and brightest body in our solar system. It looks small because it is very far away from the Earth. The Sun is about 150 million kilometers away from the Earth. It gives us light and warmth. The Sun rises in the East and sets in the West.

The Moon

The Moon is the second brightest object that we see in the sky. Unlike the Sun, the Moon is not a star. The Moon is the Earth's natural satellite. It does not have any light of its own. There is no air or water on the Moon. As a result, no life exists there.

The Moon appears to change its shape every night. The different shapes of the Moon that we see from the Earth are called 'phases of the Moon'.

The pictures below show the different phases of the Moon.

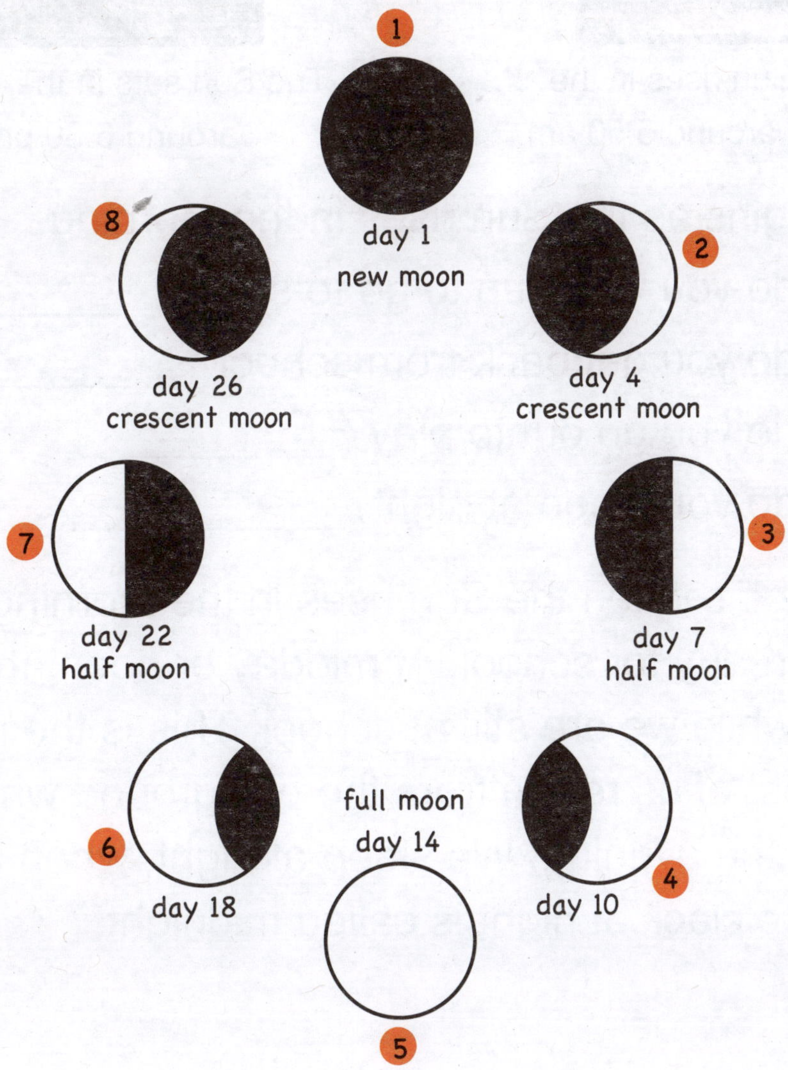

Day and Night

Explore

4 am   6 am   8 am   10 am   noon   2 pm   4 pm   6 pm   8 pm

Daytime

The Sun rises in the East at around 5.50 am.

The Sun sets in the West at around 6.30 pm.

The day begins as the Sun rises in the morning.

What time do you wake up to go to school? __________

What time do you get back from school? __________

What time do you go out to play? __________

What time do you sleep at night? __________

The day begins when the Sun rises in the morning. We wake up and get ready for school. At midday or noon, the clock strikes 12, while we are still at school. This is the middle of the day. Most of us return from the playground when the Sun sets in the evening. We sleep at night, when it is dark outside. 12 o'clock at night is called midnight.

We have day or night depending on the position of the sun. When the part of the Earth that we live on receives sunlight, we experience day. When this part of the Earth turns away from the Sun, light does not reach us. It is the night and we don't see the Sun till the next morning.

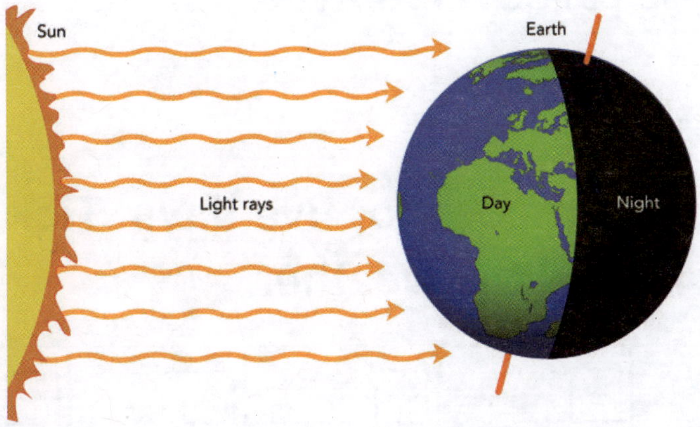

Calendar

Name three months that begin with the letter J.

________________ ________________ ________________

Name the month that has three letters. ________________

Your birthday is in ____________________.

A calendar tells us dates and days of all the twelve months of the year. Some months have thirty days while others have thirty-one. February is the shortest month with only twenty-eight or twenty-nine days. There are 12 months in a year. There are 60 seconds in a minute. There are 60 minutes in an hour. There are 24 hours in a day. There are 7 days in a week. There are about 4 weeks in every month. And 52 weeks or 365 days make up a full year.

It takes the Earth about 365 and a quarter days to go around the Sun once. We know that a year has 365 days.
Every year, the extra quarter day is carried over, and in the fourth year we add it up to get one extra day in February, known as the **leap day** (29 February). A year with an extra day in February is called a **leap year**.

Weather

Maintain a weather record for five days. Tick (✓) the correct box to record the weather.

Monday				
Tuesday				
Wednesday				
Thursday				
Friday				

The Earth has a layer of air around it called the **atmosphere**. Changes in the atmosphere, such as the presence of clouds, winds and water vapour, make a place hot or cold. This is known as the **weather**. The weather changes every day. The weather can be hot or cold, cloudy or sunny, windy or rainy. The **climate** of any place is the average weather of that place for many years. While the weather can change in a few hours, the climate of a place takes many, many years to change.

Seasons

What do you do in summer? How do you keep yourself cool and comfortable?

The weather pattern changes a few times in a year. Such changes in weather patterns are known as seasons. Seasons can be as short as two to three months or as long as six. Seasons can be hot, wet, cool or cold.

Summer, monsoon, autumn, winter and spring are the five important seasons in India. Some places, such as Pune in Maharashtra, experience the same weather throughout the year, with very slight changes. Then there are some places that do not really experience winter; for example, Chennai and Cochin in the South. As India is a vast country, different parts of the country have different seasons at the same time of the year.

Summer

In India, the summer months are usually April, May and June. The Sun is hot and bright, and the air is warm and dry. The days are longer than the nights. It is best to stay indoors and drink plenty of liquids during the hot summer days. We wear light cotton clothes to keep ourselves cool. We use fans, coolers and air conditioners to stay comfortable in summer.

Rainy Season

Cool winds from the sea bring rain clouds in July and August. The rainy season is known as monsoon. It is the wettest season of the year. Sometimes we see a rainbow after it rains. Farmers pray for rain. Rains make crops grow well. Rainwater fills up the rivers and lakes.

Autumn

Autumn is the period just before the onset of winter, generally September and October. Trees shed their leaves in this season. It is neither too hot nor too cold in autumn.

Winter

In India, November, December and January are the winter months. The Sun shines but not too brightly. Sometimes there is fog and mist. It snows on the mountain tops. We enjoy hot food and drinks in winter.

Spring

Spring is a very short season in our country. Flowers bloom during spring. The air feels fresh. It is neither hot nor cold. Spring is also known as the 'queen of all seasons'. February and March are the spring months. People go for picnics and outings during this period as the weather is very pleasant.

Learn More

Read the weather report in the daily newspaper.

Self Check

- The Sun, the Moon and the stars are all heavenly bodies. ☐
- The Sun gives us heat and light. It rises in the East and sets in the West. ☐
- The Moon moves around the Earth and appears to change its shape. ☐
- We have day or night depending on the position of the Sun. ☐
- The weather changes every day. ☐
- The climate of any place is the average weather condition of that place. ☐

- Changes in weather patterns are known as seasons. ☐
- Summer, monsoon, autumn, winter and spring are the five important seasons in India. ☐

____

____

Practice

1. Fill in the blanks to complete the sentences.

(a) Changes in the ____________ are known as weather.

(b) When a place has the same weather for a long period of time, it is known as the ___________of that place.

(c) There are ___________ seasons in a year in India.

(d) The coldest season is ___________.

(e) There are ____________ days in a week.

2. Write T for true and F for false statements.

(a) The Moon is a great ball of fire, just like the Sun. ☐

(b) The Sun is the star nearest to the Earth. ☐

(c) Life exists on the Moon. ☐

(d) The Moon changes its shape every day. ☐

(e) There are four weeks in a year. ☐

3. Answer the following questions.

(a) What are heavenly bodies?

(b) What do we get from the Sun?

(c) What are seasons? Name the seasons we experience in India.

(d) Farheen drew a diagram of the Moon she saw one night. After three nights, she drew another diagram of what the Moon looked like then. Why does the Moon look different on different nights?

(i) The Moon appears to change its shape and size every day.

(ii) The Moon comes closer to the Earth every day.

(iii) The Moon's light changes every day.

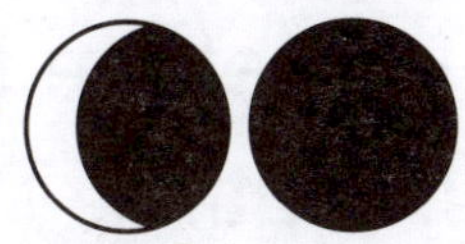

(iv) Both (ii) and (iii)

(e) The Earth has ___________ natural satellite.

(i) one (ii) two (ii) sixteen (iv) eight

4. Critical Thinking

(a) Where do stars go during the day? Discuss.

(b) What would happen if the Sun suddenly disappeared?

5. Social Emotional Skills

It is the rainy season and you and your friend get wet in the rain. Soon after, your friend starts to sneeze and has a fever. How will you help your friend?

6. Creativity

What if the wind, rain, or sunshine could talk? What do you think they would say, and how would they describe there jobs?

18 The Earth

Explore

Observe a globe. Find out what the different colours on it indicate.

Planet the Earth is our home. It is beautiful. The Earth is shaped like an orange. It goes around the Sun and gets light and heat from it.

The Earth is made up of land and water. Land covers one-fourth of the surface of the Earth. The remaining three-fourths are covered with water.

the Earth

Factastic!

A globe is an accurate world map. Like the planet the Earth, the globe is also shaped like an orange. All the countries are shown just the way they appear on the Earth.

Land Forms

Circle Time

Have you ever visited any hill station? What did you see there? Discuss in the class.

Plains are flat lands. Many famous cities are in the plains. Crops grow well located in the plains. Some parts of plains are covered with forests. The plains are usually hot in summers and cold in winters. Many people live in the plains.

plains

Deserts are large areas of land that are very dry and are usually covered with sand. There is very little water in a desert, and so very few trees grow there. Most commonly seen plants in deserts are cacti.

desert

Hills and **mountains** are elevated rocky areas. They are much higher than the plains. Fewer people live in hilly regions than in the plains.

High hills are known as mountains. It is very cold during winters in the mountains. High mountain peaks are usually covered in snow. As the snow starts to melt, rivers form in the mountains.

hills

Valleys are the lowlands between mountains or hills. There are often thick forests in valleys. The land in a valley is fertile and good for growing crops. The climate is very pleasant. Valleys are usually densely populated.

valley

plateau

A highland that is flat on top is known as a **plateau**. A plateau is also known as a table land as its top looks like the top of a table.
A plateau is usually rocky.

An **island** is land that is completely surrounded by water on all sides. The largest island in the world is Greenland. Some islands are their own countries, such as Cuba, Iceland and Madagascar. The Andaman and Nicobar Islands and Lakshadweep Islands are a part of India.

Water

Look at the pictures and write how water is being used.

____

____

____

____

Sources of Water

Plants and animals need water to survive. Rivers, lakes, ponds, wells, seas and oceans are different sources of water.

A small body of water is known as a **pond**. Ponds generally dry up during the summers.

A large body of water is called a **lake**. It is surrounded by land on all sides.

The water we see on the surface of the Earth is known as **surface water.** We build dams and canals to use this surface water.

Some of the rainwater is absorbed or seeps into the ground. This is known as **ground water**.

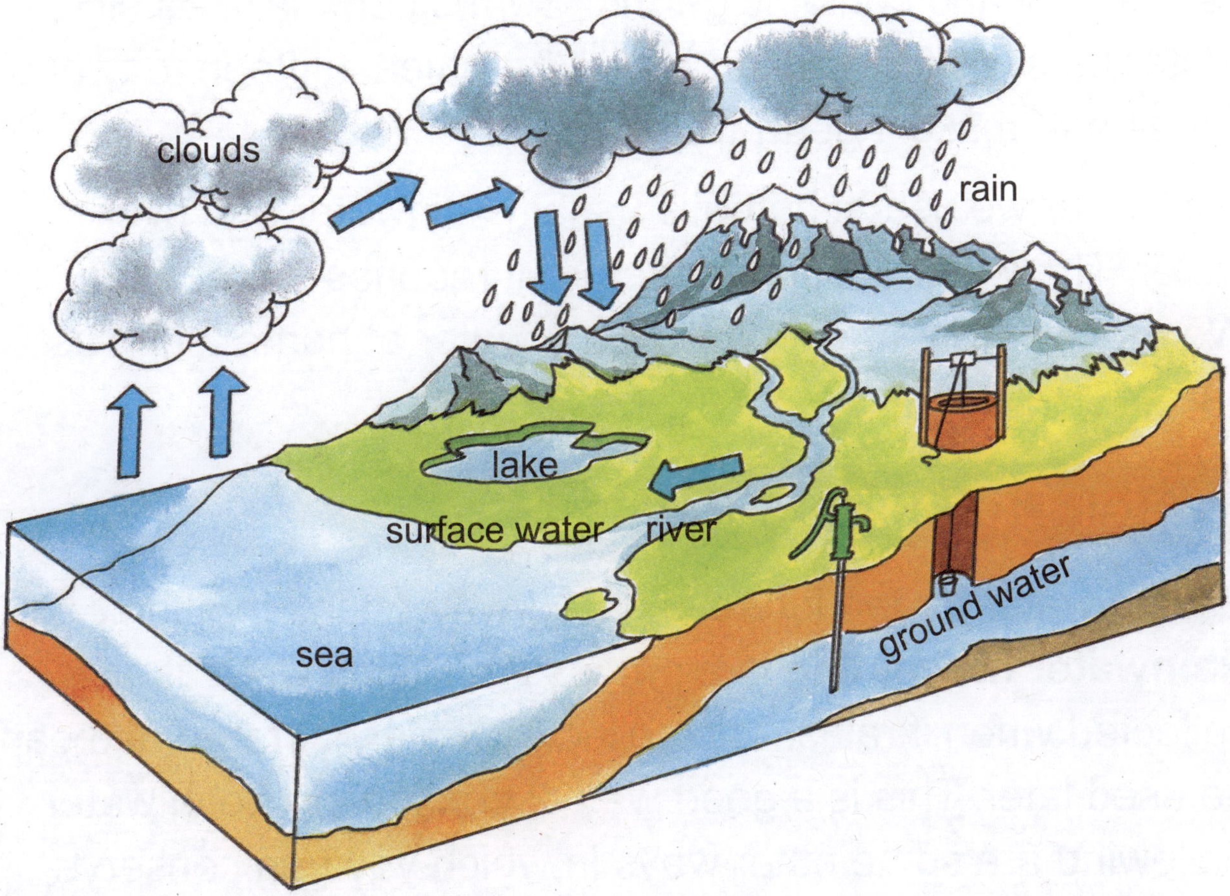

A big channel of flowing water is known as a **river**. Rivers start from the mountains and then flow down to the plains. As they reach the plains, they slow down. There are many cities and towns along the banks of rivers. Rivers empty out into the sea. **Seas** and **oceans** are very large bodies of water.

All sources of water depend on rain. Therefore, rain is the main source of water. When it rains, rainwater collects in lakes, ponds and rivers. A large part of it also seeps through the soil and collects under the ground.

Sea water is too salty to drink. We rely on fresh water (or non-salty water) from lakes, ponds, wells and rivers for domestic purposes. But we cannot drink this water directly as it is dirty and contains germs. Germs can make us sick. Water must be filtered and boiled for at least fifteen to twenty minutes to make it germ-free.

The water we use at home is usually rainwater and river water. The water is cleaned before it reaches our homes. We use different methods to purify water at home, such as boiling and filtration.

Water Conservation

Saving water for the future is called water conservation. **Rainwater harvesting** is a process by which water is collected when it rains. The collected water is stored and can be used later. This is a good way of conserving fresh water. Following are some other ways in which you can conserve water:

- Store rainwater in tanks, buckets or bottles and use it later for cleaning and washing things in the house.
- Do not keep the water running when you brush your teeth.
- Use a bucket of water instead of a shower for taking a bath.

Circle Time

What are the different things you can do to prevent air pollution?

Air

Air is all around us. We can feel it, even though we can't see it. Air is a mixture of gases, moisture and particles. All living beings need air to breathe. Air contains small particles of dust. When we dry clothes, the water in them evaporates into the air as water vapour.

Air Pollution

With more and more cars on the roads, and more factories and industries, air turns impure or polluted. This contamination of air is called air pollution.

Polluted air causes lung and skin diseases, and is harmful to birds, animals and trees as well. There are germs in the air that could make us ill. We must always cover our mouth when we cough, yawn or sneeze so that we do not spread germs.

Following are some things you can do to prevent air pollution and keep the air clean:

- Plant trees to keep the air fresh and clean.
- If you are going to a place close by, ride a bicycle instead of riding in a car.

- During Diwali, decorate your house with *diyas* instead of bursting harmful firecrackers.

Moving Air

We can feel the air when it moves. Moving air is known as wind. A gentle wind is known as **breeze**. When the wind is strong and is blowing very fast, it is known as **storm**.
A strong wind can blow away things and can cause a lot of damage. A very strong wind is also known as **gale**.

breeze wind storm gale

Factastic!

A wind gauge is used for recording the speed and direction of wind. It is also known as an anemometer.

Learn More

Mohan stores water in tanks. He lives on a farm and needs a lot of water every day. What do you think he does with all the water?

Self Check

- We all live on the planet the Earth. ☐
- Land covers one-fourth and water covers the remaining three-fourth of the surface of the Earth. ☐
- The surface of the Earth has plains, deserts, hills, mountains, valleys and plateaus. ☐
- The water on the surface of the Earth, in rivers, ponds, lakes, seas and oceans, is known as surface water. ☐
- The water that seeps into the ground is called ground water. ☐
- We must drink clean germ-free water. ☐
- We must takes steps to save water. ☐
- Air is all around us. We can feel the air but we cannot see it. ☐
- All living beings need air to breathe. ☐

____

____

Practice

1. Fill in the blanks to complete the sentences.

(a) High hills are known as ____________.

(b) Moving air is known as ____________.

(c) Land covers ____________ of the Earth's surface.

(d) ____________ are the lowlands between mountains.

(e) Ponds, lakes and rivers are sources of ____________ water.

(f) Rivers flow into ____________ and oceans.

2. Correct the following statements.

(a) The Sun goes around the Earth.

(b) A gentle wind is known as storm.

(c) A small body of water is called a lake.

(d) We can drink water directly from rivers.

3. Answer the following questions.

(a) What are valleys?

(b) Name two sources each of ground and surface water.

(c) Differentiate between the following:

(i) valley and plateau

(ii) breeze and gale

(iii) groundwater and surface water

(d) Mrs Chauhan reuses water which was used to wash vegetables, to water plants.
She is practising _________of water.

(i) pollution (ii) conservation

(iii) evaporation (ii) condensation

(e) Select the odd one.

(i) breeze (ii) storm

(iii) gale (ii) rain

4. **Critical Thinking**

(a) Is our the Earth moving or stationary? Discuss.

(b) Why is it important to keep waterbodies clean? Discuss.

5. **Social Emotional Skills**

How do you feel when you see water being wasted? What can you do to stop wastage of this precious resource in your community?

6. **Creativity**

Make a model of the Earth using a ball.

Cross-curricular Project

Our Environment

Our natural world comprises our environment. It includes all living and non-living organisms. Birds, animals, plants, humans, rivers, mountains, etc. all form our environment.

1. **Our earth is full of beautiful natural wonders. Some of them are:**

Living Roots Bridge (Meghalaya)

Aerial bridges made out of the roots of rubber fig trees.

Gandikota Canyon (Andhra Pradesh)

A natural formation carved by the Pennar River.

Loktak Lake (Manipur)

A freshwater lake with floating islands.

Yana Caves (Karnataka)

These caves are natural ancient limestone rock formations.

2. **Have you seen or do you know of a place which is as beautiful as the ones shown in previous page?**

Paste a photo of that place and write a few lines about it.

Where is the place?

Why is it special?

Best time to visit the place

3. Celebrating World Animal Day

Your school is celebrating the World Animal Day. Which animal will you choose for your poster and what will you write on your poster?

WORLD ANIMAL DAY

SAVE ANIMALS BECAUSE...

____

____

____

____

4. Our environment is getting polluted every day. This is affecting our plants, animals, soil and air. What can we do to save our Mother Earth? In groups, make 5 stickers to show ways in which we can save our planet. For example: